PRESENTING
Richard Peck

TUSAS 554

Twayne's United States Authors Series
Young Adult Authors

Patricia J. Campbell, General Editor

The Young Adult Authors books seek to meet the
need for critical studies of fiction for young adults.
Each volume examines the life and work of one
author, helping both teachers and readers of young
adult literature to understand better the writers they
have read with such pleasure and fascination.

PRESENTING
Richard Peck

Donald R. Gallo

Twayne Publishers • Boston
A Division of G. K. Hall & Co.

Presenting Richard Peck
Donald R. Gallo

FRANKLIN PIERCE COLLEGE
LIBRARY

Copyright 1989 by G. K. Hall & Co. RINDGE, NH 03461
All rights reserved.
Published by Twayne Publishers
A Division of G. K. Hall & Co.
70 Lincoln Street
Boston, Massachusetts 02111

Photographs and captions kindly provided by Richard Peck and Donald R. Gallo
Book production by Gabrielle B. McDonald
Copyediting supervised by Barbara Sutton

Typeset in 10/13 Century Schoolbook
by Compositors Corporation, Cedar Rapids, Iowa

Printed on permanent/durable acid-free paper
and bound in the United States of America

Library of Congress Cataloging–in–Publication Data
Gallo, Donald R.
 Presenting Richard Peck / Donald R. Gallo.
  p. cm.—(Twayne's United States authors series ; TUSAS
554. Young adult authors)
 Bibliography: p.
 Includes index.
 Summary: Discusses the life and work of Richard Peck, examining his essays, poetry, and novels for children, young adults, and adults.
 ISBN 0-8057-8209-5 (alk. paper)
 1. Peck, Richard, 1934- —Criticism and interpretation.
[1. Peck, Richard, 1934- —Criticism and interpretation.
2. American literature—History and criticism.] I. Title.
II. Series: Twayne's United States authors series ; TUSAS 554.
III. Series: Twayne's United States authors series. Young adult authors.
PS3566.E2526Z68 1989
818'.5409—dc20
            89-32346
            CIP
            AC

Contents

Preface

Waiting for the distinguished author to end his question-and-answer session, the middle-aged librarian sat straight-backed in the center of the first row clutching a pristine copy of *Something for Joey*. A few rows behind her, with a dog-eared paperback copy of *A Day No Pigs Would Die* resting on her knee, sat a young junior high school English teacher. Both were waiting to get the speaker's autograph. When they presented their books to the author, both were surprised. The author wasn't.

For years, Richard Peck has been mistaken for both Richard E. Peck and for Robert Newton Peck. Recently Richard Peck received a package of letters from students in a junior high school, sent by a teacher. Half of them were written to Richard Peck and half to Robert Newton Peck. "She didn't know the difference," Richard remarks. "A Peck is a Peck."

To set the record straight: Richard Peck is not the author of *Something for Joey*, the emotional, true story of John Cappelletti, the Los Angeles Rams football player, and his younger brother's struggle against leukemia. Nor did Richard Peck write the popular Soup series or the memorable and widely taught *A Day No Pigs Would Die*. "I wish I *had* written it," he says. This book is about Richard Peck, the author of *Father Figure*, *Remembering the Good Times*, *Princess Ashley*, *Amanda/Miranda*, and the Blossom Culp supernatural stories, as well as the essayist, anthologist, poet, and popular lecturer. Make no mistake about it.

Donald R. Gallo

Central Connecticut State University

Acknowledgments

Books of this kind often begin with a word of thanks to the subject, without whom the work could never have been written. That acknowledgment is even more necessary with this book. When he was told that he was to be the subject of one of the volumes in Twayne's Young Adult Authors Series, Richard Peck's first response was negative. For a variety of reasons he did not like the idea of being scrutinized and limned. "I'm neither able nor willing to be as cooperative as you'd need," he wrote. He promised to stonewall.

But once he accepted the idea, he was more than cooperative, and he consented to an interview in his New York City apartment. Although he was very nervous at first, he talked freely and candidly for over four hours and then agreed to a second interview. That second one lasted nearly seven hours! In addition, he provided me with copies of hard to obtain reviews, two new short stories, the British edition of one of his adult novels, and a previously unpublished poem. He also graciously read a preliminary draft of three major chapters of the manuscript for this book, corrected inaccurate details, and added previously unknown information. Thanks are also due Richard Peck for granting permission to reproduce "Early Admission" along with lines from "The Geese," and other lines of verse included in the poetry chapter. This book undoubtedly could not have been written without Richard Peck's cooperation, and I am extremely grateful for his generosity.

Thanks also to Suzanne Murphy, Paula Heller, and Teresa Roberts for providing me access to the files on Richard Peck in the publicity offices of Dell Publishing Company. Those files of reviews and articles on Peck's novels saved me countless hours of library research. And for assistance in locating obscure sources, I am grateful to librarians in the public libraries of West Hartford, Hartford, and Simsbury, Connecticut, as well as in the Curriculum Lab and the Inter-library Loan department at Central Connecticut State University.

To Louann Reid I owe special thanks for her insightful critiques and valuable suggestions on preliminary drafts of this book. And I am grateful to Patty Campbell and Athenaide Dallett for their patience as well as their clear directions and helpful advice in preparing as well as editing the manuscript.

Chronology

1934   Richard Peck born 5 April in Decatur, Illinois.

1950   Visits a distant relative in New York City.

1951   Is challenged by Miss Franklin in senior English.

1952   Enters DePauw University, planning to be a teacher.

1954   Sails to England on the *Ile de France* and spends junior year at Exeter University.

1956   Graduates from DePauw and enters the army; spends two years in Germany as a company clerk and a chaplain's assistant.

1958   Enters graduate school at Southern Illinois University at Carbondale; serves as teaching assistant in English Department. Continues teaching there as instructor in English after receiving master's degree.

1961   Teaches English at Glenbrook North High School in Northbrook, Illinois.

1963   Works as textbook editor for Scott, Foresman and Company, Chicago.

1965   Begins teaching English and education at Hunter College and Hunter College High School in New York City. *Old Town, A Complete Guide: Strolling, Shopping, Supping, Sipping*, with Norman Strasma.

1966   *Edge of Awareness: Twenty-Five Contemporary Essays*, with Ned E. Hoopes.

1967 *Open Court Correlated Language Arts Program.*

1969 Serves one-year fellowship in Washington, D.C., as assistant director of the Council for Basic Education.

1970 *Sounds and Silences: Poetry for Now.*

1971 *Mindscapes: Poems for the Real World.* Resigns from teaching, intending to become a novelist.

1972 *A Consumer's Guide to Educational Innovations,* with Mortimer Smith and George Weber. *Don't Look and It Won't Hurt.*

1973 *Dreamland Lake. Through a Brief Darkness. The Creative Word,* vol. 2, with Stephen N. Judy. *Urban Studies: A Research Paper Casebook. Leap into Reality: Essays for Now.*

1974 *Representing Super Doll. Transitions: A Literary Paper Casebook.*

1975 *The Ghost Belonged to Me.*

1976 *Are You in the House Alone? Pictures That Storm Inside My Head: Poems for the Inner You.*

1977 *Ghosts I Have Been. Monster Night at Grandma's House* (illustrated by Don Freeman).

1978 *Father Figure.*

1979 *Secrets of the Shopping Mall.*

1980 *Amanda/Miranda.*

1981 *Close Enough to Touch. New York Time.*

1983 *The Dreadful Future of Blossom Culp. This Family of Women.*

1985 *Remembering the Good Times.*

1986 *Blossom Culp and the Sleep of Death.*

1987 *Princess Ashley.*

1988 *Those Summer Girls I Never Met.*

1. The Person

Richard Peck is a paradox. He reveres the study of Latin, yet he writes novels that are unencumbered by difficult vocabulary. He is a writer who by tradition and the necessities of the trade must labor alone facing a silent page, yet he travels 70,000 miles a year to meet and talk personally with librarians, teachers, and teenagers. Although he left the teaching profession in 1971, he continues to see himself as a teacher as well as a writer. While he jealously guards his personal privacy, he constantly delves into the feelings and experiences of teenagers for insights into attitudes and experiences that he can use in his books. He is angry about a lot of things, yet even his serious novels are filled with humor. Although in his speeches and in his published essays he is extremely critical of contemporary teenagers as a group, he is unusually supportive and concerned about today's adolescents, continually striving to lift them up through his books and public presentations. And while he is one of the most well-known and most highly respected writers of young adult novels, he does not see himself as a worthy subject of a book such as this.

In addition to those conflicting characteristics, Richard Peck is a tall, trim, always neatly dressed, intense, tightly wound individual who is dedicated to his craft. In appearance and in behavior, if not in heritage, he is a gentleman in the fullest sense of the word: gracious,

honorable, independent, and charming. He is also a master of the
one-liner, as you will see throughout this book, for no one else can describe his often jaundiced views of schools, books, parents, kids, and
the world better than he does in witty, insightful, sometimes well-
rehearsed statements.

Richard Peck entered the field of young adult books virtually at
the beginning of the modern era. When he gave up his teaching job in
1971, S. E. Hinton's *The Outsiders* and Robert Lipsyte's *The Con-
tender* had been in paperback for just three years and Paul Zindel's
The Pigman for two years; *Go Ask Alice* was just being printed—all of
them cutting a new and exciting path in the publishing world. No one
had yet heard of Robert Newton Peck or M. E. Kerr or Robert
Cormier. Or Richard Peck.

In the years since his first published novel, Richard Peck has
grown along with the field of young adult books to become one of its
top authors, while his writing and his speaking have been key factors
in sustaining and advancing that field. When the Young Adult Services Division of the American Library Association published their
list of the Best of the Best Books 1970–82, only two of the seventy-
five authors had more than two books on that list: Richard Peck and
Ursula K. LeGuin had three titles each.[1] In fact, eight of Peck's novels have been named Best Young Adult Books of the Year by the
American Library Association. In a 1988 survey of forty-one past
and present officers of the Assembly on Literature for Adolescents
of the National Council of Teachers of English to determine the
hundred most important authors of novels for teenagers, Richard
Peck received more votes than all the others except S. E. Hinton and
Paul Zindel.[2]

While some writers view themselves as being more important than
others think they are, the opposite is true of Richard Peck. When ap-
proached for an interview as this book was in its formative stage,
Peck recoiled at having been singled out for such an honor. Although
concern about his personal privacy was no doubt part of his concern,
he revealingly said: "I don't think I'm the stuff of biography."[3] Nor
does he care to ponder his place of importance in the publishing
world. "I don't think about who's best," he declares. "I think about
how this field is accumulating more and more good writers." Ex-

panding on that, Peck adds: "Gore Vidal said: 'Everytime a friend of mine succeeds, I die a little.' I don't like that. . . . I think one book feeds another. I think Judy Blume in many ways is the mother of us all, because she kept young people reading whose schools were not keeping them reading."

"I really do like the concept of colleagues," he says. Which colleagues, then, does he respect and admire most? S. E. Hinton is the first he mentions: "She does the kind of books I could never write, or believe in. She knew without knowing. Most of us came from something else; she came from adolescence!" Then M. E. Kerr: "A stylist. I like stylists." And of course Robert Cormier. *The Chocolate War* is the first book Peck recommends in his recent speeches to teachers. He greatly admires Terry Davis's *Vision Quest*: "Still one of the best novels I've *ever* read." Peck also singles out Chris Crutcher, Bruce Brooks, and Michael French from among the younger writers in the field.

Peck's praise is without the slightest hint of jealousy or envy. "I want people to look up to them, not down," he avers. "You don't learn anything by reading and saying, 'I could do better than that.'" Putting it another way, Peck says about these admirable books: "I wish I had written them, [but] I know I wouldn't have written them, so I'm glad somebody did. These books give me permission."

For some authors writing is an end in itself. Others write for the prestige or for money. Although his writing has brought him material comfort as well as considerable recognition, Richard Peck writes because he feels driven to do so. He sees today's teenagers lost in a focusless world, manipulated by peer pressure, mesmerized by shallow television programs, unsupervised by parents too busy or too afraid to take charge, at sea in schools with wishy-washy curriculums and undemanding administrators. Peck reaches out to those few students who will read independently, hoping his messages will get across once readers are attracted by the entertainment value of his novels. "Writing remains the act of reaching out in the dark, hoping for a hand to hold," he states.[4]

Writing books with characters who can serve as companions as well as role models for teenagers, Peck says: "I write for these people whose own parents haven't seen them for days."[5] He doesn't write for students who are leaders of the student council or the captains of athletic teams; instead he aims his books, as he puts it, at students on the edge of the crowd, young people who are capable of acting independently. Most of his lead characters as well as the young people he believes he writes for are not team players; "they're lonely, long-distance runners,"[6] characters who tend to be "self-reliant, semi-loner[s], standing at the edge of the action—observing it with a keen ironic eye,"[7] as they gather strength to launch themselves once the novel ends.[8] And although he has written novels that fit into a variety of topical categories, one theme dominates them all: "YOU WILL NEVER BEGIN TO GROW UP UNTIL YOU START TO ACT AND THINK INDEPENDENTLY OF YOUR PEERS."[9]

Peck differs from most of his colleagues also by the age at which he began his writing career. S. E. Hinton started publishing her novels as a teenager. M. E. Kerr began writing right out of college, although she did not write for young adults until much later in her career. Robert Cormier did not publish his first young adult novel until he was fifty years old, but he had been a newspaper writer for the previous twenty-five years and had published short stories since his college years. Peck did not write a line of fiction until he was thirty-seven years old. "I wonder what would have happened if I had gotten started earlier," he ponders. "I don't begrudge the time getting ready, because I think I needed it." The preparation paid off, for Richard Peck has never written a novel that has failed to sell or to attract attention. In fact, as of the date of this writing, every one of his fifteen novels for young adults is still in print.

Peck differs in other ways also from most of his writing colleagues. While most writers spend their days behind their typewriters and word-processors, he spends approximately one-fourth of his time traveling to more than sixty schools and libraries each year to talk with young people, their teachers, and librarians. He has also written and published in a wider variety of literary forms than most young adult authors: poems, essays, reviews, and newspaper pieces, as well as three successful adult novels and a picture book for children, in addition to compiling and editing three poetry anthologies and two essay collections.

When asked what makes his books better than others available to teenagers today, Peck at first deflects the question, reluctant to compare his work with others. But when asked, What is your greatest strength as a young adult author?, his answer comes quickly and easily:

> The use of research. Not library research. But sitting at home, imagining what it might be like, then going out and seeking what it *is* like, and then being able to put into the book something that will make the reader write back and say, "Do you live around here? How did you know we wore that, or said that, or did that?"

Critics have been consistent in their praise of Peck's witty and realistic dialogue, as well as his adept plotting and his empathy for teenagers' problems. In reviewing *The Dreadful Future of Blossom Culp*, for example, Marilou Sorenson observes: "His descriptions are vivid and succinct, and he spoofs the 'now' generation with their own slang. . . . And the dialogue is sharp and poignant."[10] A *Kirkus* reviewer writing about *Princess Ashley* lauds Peck for "deftly captur[ing] the evolving concerns of 15- and 16-year-olds—their speech, anxieties, and shifting relationships with parents and peers."[11] Writing about *Close Enough to Touch*, Mary K. Chelton applauds Peck's "unerring observance of adolescent mores."[12] Responding to that same novel, a reviewer in *Publishers Weekly* lauds Peck's "grace and wit and—most of all—understanding of confused teenagers."[13] His "beautifully crafted language, subtle humor and insight into the teenagers' world" as well as his "finely honed style" are extolled in a review of *Remembering the Good Times*.[14] Writing of *Princess Ashley* in *School Library Journal*, Denise A. Anton notes Peck's "sensitive and insightful view of teenage life" and the "expertly drawn and totally believable" characters,[15] while Evie Wilson, in *Voice of Youth Advocates*, notes the "timely issues, characters of depth and feeling, and life-like scenarios which stun the reader with the power of their reality."[16]

This is a writer of consistently good books for young people. What factors have shaped him and influenced his style, focused his attention, and earned his praise or evoked his condemnation?

Although he makes his home in New York City, Richard Peck's roots are in central Illinois, a place whose influence is evident in several of his novels as well as in his attitude about what's important in life. Born on 5 April 1934, he grew up in a white frame house on Dennis Avenue next to Fairview Park in Decatur until he went away to college at the age of eighteen. Peck characterizes Decatur as "a smug, stratified, endlessly various town that thought it was a city."[17] Located between what they called Little Egypt of southern Illinois and the big city of Chicago to the north, the residents, Peck claims, "came to the logical conclusion that we were the center of the earth."[18] This Midwestern town would later provide Peck with the setting for several of his novels: in *Representing Super Doll* and *Dreamland Lake* it is called Dunthorpe, with Fairview Park becoming Dreamland Park; and in the Blossom Culp novels, Decatur as it was in the early 1900s is called Bluff City.

Unlike many children today who come from single-parent families or from homes where they receive little attention or supervision from adults, Peck notes, he was surrounded by a loving, caring extended family, including his maternal grandmother Flossie Mae Gray and her four sisters, Pearl, Mura, Maude, and Ozena, all with roots in the rich farmland of the Midwest. His great-grandfather William Gray, an Irish immigrant, had acquired a farm in western Illinois in 1852 that he passed down to his son John who farmed it until 1964. That prosperous Walnut Grove Farm, Peck recalls fondly, contained "a fine, high house with long, deep porches standing in a vast lawn of enormous trees and mounded flower beds. The views ran to the level line of the horizon. . . . The weedless garden rows ran straight as a die from the fence line, burdened with bounty."[19] This same house provided the setting for his children's book, *Monster Night at Grandma's House*.

His mother, Virginia Gray, trained as a dietician, made an art of home cooking. From his growing-up years during World War II, Peck recalls his father bringing home the products of his hunting and fishing trips: pheasants, catfish, and croppie. Live chickens from his grandparents' farm were dispatched in the back yard as needed, an act that Peck recreated vividly in the opening scene of *Representing Super Doll*. When meat was rationed, calves and hogs that had been raised on the farms of the Pecks' rural relatives provided ample reserves for Richard's family.

Wayne M. Peck, Richard's father, was raised on an Illinois farm. During his teenage years he dropped out of school and hopped freight trains to the Dakotas where he joined in the wheat harvest. When the First World War raged in Europe, he went off to fight in France, returning partially disabled with a shattered left shoulder. Back home, he was displeased to find that life had changed, and so he often reminisced about his youth. Thus, from his father, Richard Peck declares, "I learned nostalgia as an art form." Young Richard thought: "He was a farm boy. Of course, if you didn't grow up on a farm you wouldn't have had a childhood." And so Richard Peck, growing up in town, believed that he had been "born after the party was over."

Unable to farm, Wayne Peck settled in town where he ran a Phillips 66 gas station during Richard's youth. And instead of wearing a white shirt and driving off to work in a Plymouth sedan each day as Richard remembers other fathers doing, his father wore coveralls and roared away on a Harley-Davidson motorcycle.

In his father's gas station, twelve-year-old boys rolled their newspapers, and from them Richard learned vocabulary beyond his years. He was also privy to the conversations of older men, since his father ran his gas station, Peck notes, "like a club where elderly men—old truckers and farmers and railroaders—hung out, telling tales." Their stories were honed "with years of retelling and flavored . . . with tobacco juice."[20] At the Walnut Grove Farm, Richard listened in on stories of his grandparents' and great-aunts' Victorian pasts—"voices from the previous century."[21] At home, he was privy to the stories of his aunts and uncles, especially of Aunt Rozella, who lived with them for the first fifteen years of Richard's life. From all these people Richard Peck says he learned style. And the phrasing of his great-aunts later provided him with the voice of Blossom Culp.

The most colorful of his relatives was his great-uncle Miles: an octogenarian carpenter "who terrorized the town in a Model A Ford fitted out with a carpentry box where the rumble seat had been." Peck remembers his rogue relative as "the worst snob in a town full of them."[22] He had "married often but not seriously," and had "a keen nose for scandal, and inconvenient memories of other people's pasts." Peck explains, "[H]e was as free as I hoped adults could be.

Grownups dreaded him; I sopped up his every word."[23] In addition to local history—"for the past and present were a single tapestry in his [great-uncle's] mind"[24]—Richard learned a good deal of creative language from this foul-mouthed rascal and later brought him back to life as a major character in *The Ghost Belonged to Me.*

Thus the voices and stories of these living characters remained in Richard Peck's memory until they began to appear years later as models for fictional characters in his novels. "When you write to young readers, you need the wisdom of those people at the other end of life," Peck believes. "I came to writing with an entire crew of seasoned elders on my side."[25]

Richard Peck entered kindergarten on the day Hitler's army invaded Poland in 1939. Before he was enrolled in Dennis Grade School he was already primed for a later literary life, having acquired a love for books in the lap of his mother. Peck maintains, "I fell easy prey to teacher and librarians. . . . My teachers, first and last, betrayed no interest in my ideas." What was important to his teachers, Peck remembers, was "the format of grammar, and later Latin. The symmetry of sentences, the shapes of paragraphs. The sense of words, and their sounds."[26]

The war, Peck notes, suited him quite well. It gave adults a lot to talk about at home, things they didn't all agree on. From those disagreements, Peck says he learned viewpoint, a novelist's stock-in-trade. In school, discipline became more militaristic. Fascinating new words—such as *blitzkrieg* and *kamikaze*—came to light; and names of foreign places were identified on maps of the world, all of which appealed to young Richard's desire to move beyond the safe streets of Decatur. The real world was out there somewhere; the exciting things were happening someplace else. Decatur wasn't the center of the universe.

An only child until third grade, Richard acquired a sister—Cheryl. She, too, became a writer, working her way up in the newspaper business in Decatur then leaving her job to complete a master's degree in English while working with a group filming the restoration of the Abraham Lincoln house in Springfield, Illinois. But back in their youth, Peck says, "I was the typical older kid; she was the typical younger. I conformed; she questioned. I recorded; she rebelled."[27]

Richard Peck, his sister Cheryl Peck, and their mother Mrs. Wayne Peck—1985.
Reproduced courtesy of Richard Peck.

Richard never rebelled. Recalling his years at Woodrow Wilson Junior High School as a time when students respected and obeyed teachers without question, Richard never went to school without his homework completed. "I did homework out of fear, not goodness," he says. "From junior high on, I thought that the only safe way to a scholarship was a string of A's on the report card." Through his after-school paper route, along with his friend Chick Wolfe, he learned responsibility. And from Miss Van Dyke's Fortnightly Dancing Class he learned proper social behavior. Peck concludes: "I touched all these bases because from early times I really thought you had a lot of dues to pay before they'd let you into adulthood. For middle-class kids, it was very much that kind of era, but I think I believed it more than most."

In Stephen Decatur High School, with the secret goal of becoming a writer, Richard studied hard, aiming for membership in the National Honor Society and a scholarship so that he could attend a private college. In retrospect, Peck believes that his schooling laid the groundwork for a novelist: "history, Latin, and geography: something to say, how to say it, and somewhere to set the story."[28]

But one serious problem existed for Peck: there were no role models. Young Richard noticed that all of the writers he and his fellow students were required to study in school were dead and none had come from Central Illinois. How then could he, Richard, ever hope to be a writer? Then one day during his junior year, his English teacher, Miss Gorham, announced that the sister of Vachel Lindsay, a poet from Illinois, would read his poetry at nearby Millikin University. "I went that night to see what a poet's sister looked like," Peck recalls. Not only did he hear Olive Lindsay Wakefield recite her brother's cadenced poetry but he also later visited the Lindsay family home where the lonely old sister lived before it became a museum.[29]

During Richard's high school years he was invited to visit a distant relative in New York City during the summer of his sixteenth year. Longing to explore other places, "I raked yards and shoveled snow for a chair-car ticket on the Pennsylvania Railroad and was on my way," he remembers. It was a breakthrough experience for him. As he tells it: "It came as quite a relief to me that the outside world was really there and somewhat better than the movies. I began to explore the streets of New York and plumb the depths of the subway system all the way to Coney Island. It occurred to me that this was the place I'd been homesick for all along, this place and London."[30] Fifteen more years would pass before Richard Peck made his way back to New York.

Managing to earn good grades, Richard was inducted into the National Honor Society, proud of his academic success as he entered his senior year. But between Richard and college stood Miss Franklin. There was no way to avoid the notorious Miss F. at Stephen Decatur High School, for if you were college-bound, you took senior English from her. Peck recalls that on the first day of his senior year she assured the class, with dramatic emphasis, that she had the power to get them into the colleges of their choice—or keep them out.[31] And he believed her.

Accustomed to receiving A's on his English compositions, Richard was surprised to find no grade on the first paper he wrote for Miss Franklin. Instead she had written: "'NEVER EXPRESS YOURSELF AGAIN ON MY TIME. FIND A MORE INTERESTING TOPIC.'" Peck explains what happened next:

Well, I was seventeen. I didn't know what a more interesting topic than me would be. I actually went to the woman and asked, "What would a more interesting topic be?"

"Almost anything," she replied.

That led me to the library, a place I'd successfully avoided up until then, in search of subject matter that wasn't me. All these years later, I'm still searching for it. Miss F. taught us that writing isn't self-expression. Writing is communication, and you'd better have your reader far better in mind than yourself. Miss F. didn't teach Creative Writing, of course. She knew the danger of inspiration coming before grammar. She knew that without the framework for sharing, ideas are nothing.

I wasn't slated to write a line of fiction until I was thirty-seven years old, but it was Miss F. who made it possible. In the boot camp atmosphere of her classroom she taught us that the only real writing is rewriting. She taught us that deadlines are meant to be met, not extended. She taught us how to gather material more interesting than ourselves and to pin it on a page.[32]

Those things made all the difference in the world for Richard Peck.

Encouraged and supported by his parents and the Rector Scholarship he won, Richard entered DePauw University in Greencastle, Indiana, during the fall of 1952. He, like many young men at that time, was also motivated by the threat of military service: unless they had a college deferment and remained in the upper half of their college class, all able males over the age of eighteen were likely to be drafted and find themselves in Korea. Discouraged by people who said how difficult it was to make a living writing, and encouraged by the models that his teachers provided—"teachers were the people in my hometown . . . who were interested in the things I was interested in"[33]—Peck concluded that teaching was the profession that would bring him closest to the written word.[34] So he continued to work hard, planning to be a teacher, even though he really wanted to be a writer.

Richard's junior year proved to be his most important one, for he spent it in England. Having always dreamed of distant places, he sailed across the Atlantic in the fall of 1954 aboard the *Ile de France*, one of the most distinguished liners of the time. He had raised the money by working as a dishwasher at George Williams College Camp on Lake Geneva, Wisconsin, the previous summer. The *Ile de France*, he explains, was "an ocean-going Art Deco fantasy flowing with red wine even in Third Class. But I was drunk enough on the adventure of it all. The ship pitched through the gray waves while we passengers danced the nights away on slanting floors under swaying chandeliers."[35] It's an adventure he currently repeats as a lecturer and teacher of a creative writing seminar on the ships of the Royal Cruiseship Line.

In England he studied both literature and British history at Exeter University in a picturesque medieval town surrounded by rolling farmland punctuated by thatch-roofed houses. At Mardon Hall Richard acquired three scholarly friends: Henry Woolf, the university's most intelligent student, whose Jewish family had been forced out of Europe by Hitler's atrocities; David Wheatley, who had grown up in Africa and India during the fading days of the British Empire; and Arthur Dark, the son of a retired sailor from Plymouth. He later met and was looked after by the Jones family, who provided him with a second home in the town of Barnstaple near Lorna Doone's Exmoor.[36] In addition to acquiring a taste for tweeds, losing some of his American Midwestern accent, and overcoming his previous fear of speaking before a group, Richard Peck was able to explore a country that was later to be the setting for part of three of his young adult novels and one adult novel, *Amanda/Miranda*.

He returned home to focus on education courses during his senior year at DePauw. Soon after graduation, he found himself in the army, which sent him back to Europe. Expecting the worst, Peck admits that his two years in the military taught him twice as much as two years in college.[37] At a post just outside Ansbach, West Germany, Peck learned that "if you can type, spell, and improvise in midsentence, you can work in a clean, dry office near a warm stove" instead of being "knee-deep in a moist foxhole staring through barbed wire at an East German soldier who's staring back at you."[38] So he became a company clerk, whose competence with words led him into an unexpected field: ghostwriting sermons for the post's chaplains ("all denominations," Peck is quick to add). Having established himself as a ghostwriter, he was soon enlisted as chaplain's assistant and posted to Stuttgart. Today's army recruiters promise to train enlistees in practical skills such as computer programing or engine repair; in West Germany in the mid-1950s, the army promised Richard Peck nothing but gave him a lot more: it allowed him to hone his writing skills and learn to write for deadlines. In addition, Peck probably heard more confessions from his fellow soldiers than the chaplains did.[39] The problems he heard about still turn up in the novels Peck writes.

During his stint in the army and later while in graduate school, Peck continued to explore the Europe he had first encountered in his junior year abroad. He "hitch-hiked to Rome, slept in trains from Turin to Bruges, and discovered London, inch by literary inch," which led him to the belief that he has passed along to teenagers ever since: "Anyone just about to leave adolescence needs to cut himself out of the pack and be on his own." In addition, Peck was learning another valuable lesson: how to be alone—"the only way a writer can work, whenever he begins to do it in earnest," he says.[40]

After his release from the army, Richard Peck enrolled in graduate school at Southern Illinois University at Carbondale, where he served as a teaching assistant. His assignment—the first of his teaching career—was to teach writing to freshmen. Expecting to find a group of adolescents who just a few weeks before had been high school seniors, Peck found himself facing a worried group of mature adults in an evening class. "I was never again to know students this vulnerable or this punctual."[41] From that class he learned the importance of reassuring students that their experiences were valid. And the effort he put into his teaching kept him too busy to think about being a writer.[42]

For his master's thesis, Peck chose to examine Sinclair Lewis's use of European characters and settings to illuminate American life. "It's about what was happening to me when I was coming of age in Europe"—a perfect match between student and subject.

He continued to teach at Southern Illinois as an instructor in English after receiving his master's degree, doing additional graduate work at Washington University in St. Louis. But in the fall of 1961 he returned to his original plan and began teaching English in a public high school: Glenbrook North High School in the affluent Chicago suburb of Northbrook, Illinois. He was not happy with what he found.

Unlike himself as a teenager, Peck found his students to be over-indulged, self-centered, unchallenged, and rootless. They "were strongly armored with adolescent facades, peer-group allegiance, hair spray, and family money. . . . Every parent expected college entrance for his child. If there was an alternative, it was unthinkable."[43] His opinion of suburban teens has not changed to this day. But those adolescents, it turns out, provided Richard Peck with his first glimpse of the audience for whom he would eventually write best-selling novels. Glenbrook North High School itself later provided the setting for his tenth novel for young adults, *Close Enough to Touch*. But Richard Peck wasn't ready to be a writer yet. The New York publishing world was still two steps away.

After two years in Northbrook, he found employment as a text-book editor for Scott, Foresman and Company in Chicago. During his two years there, he and a college fraternity friend, Norman Strasma, wrote a lively guide to Chicago night life called *Old Town, A Complete Guide: Strolling, Shopping, Supping, Sipping*, which they published themselves in 1965. Although Peck dismisses it as a book of little consequence, it was his first significant published work.

Peck's long-standing dream of living in New York City came to fruition when he applied for and received a job teaching English and education courses at Hunter College and its laboratory school, Hunter College High School, in 1965. It was a school for academically gifted girls, located on New York City's Park Avenue. He was thirty-two years old.

Peck writes: "On the way to the first class my knees wobbled a little as they hadn't done for years. I wondered what I had to offer young geniuses flourishing in the rich cultural concrete of this world capital." It was a time of urban renewal of blighted city neighborhoods and of protests in the streets against American involvement in Vietnam. At Hunter, "There was talk of consciousness-raising in the faculty lounge. And among the students there had been Proust before puberty." Although the acceptance of paperbacks in the classroom had expanded the possibilities of the literature program, the faculty had just thrown out *To Kill a Mockingbird* because of its "white bourgeois values." In spite of this being the city of his dreams, the school "seemed too narrow a universe for me," Peck concluded.[44]

But one chance experience changed everything for the young man from rural Illinois. It was, he says, "the one scene out of my life that was a movie." At the first faculty meeting of the year, an experienced colleague, Ned Hoopes, invited Peck to "do a book" with him and gave Peck the choice of material. Within a year after arriving in the East, Richard Peck had broken into the New York publishing world with *Edge of Awareness: Twenty-Five Contemporary Essays.* "I got $730 for it, which was almost two months' pay then," he recalls. The book has since sold millions of copies and is still in print.

That first publishing experience did several things for Richard Peck. "It let me know that I was living in the same town with publishers, which I had never done before." It also enabled him to meet people in the publishing business, the most important of whom was George Nicholson, who was then a young editor and is now one of the leading figures in the business of publishing books for children and young adults. Except for his three adult books, Richard Peck has continued to publish all of his books under Nicholson's guidance. The relationship was mutually advantageous from the start: publishers were just beginning to expand their paperback lines and to look for ideas and materials that would help classroom teachers break away from the standard textbook anthologies; Richard Peck was a classroom teacher. "I learned that a teacher knew some things that publishers didn't. Well, I thought publishers knew everything! They asked: 'Would this work in the classroom?' and I said, 'This worked for me, and this is how I used it.' And they'd say, 'Well, fine.'" Because of the success of *Edge of Awareness*, the publishers commissioned Peck to compile a collection of contemporary poems for high school classes.

Meanwhile, the frustrations Peck had experienced in teaching students in suburban Illinois were even more extreme when he attempted to teach "gifted" New York City teenagers who, in Peck's judgment, felt they had nothing to learn. Nevertheless, he was an inventive, inspired teacher, doing everything he could to get students involved. One former student, employed now by a major publisher of books for young adults, remembers Peck as "a very good teacher" who was knowledgeable, committed, well-prepared, and very funny though sometimes sarcastic. Although she recalls him as being somewhat formal (he called everyone "Miss — "), her most vivid memory of her eighth-grade English class is of Richard Peck standing on a desk to recite Mark Antony's fiery funeral oration from *Julius Caesar.* While Peck believed his students were indifferent to education, his students felt they just were interested in different things than he. "He put a premium on quality literature when people were doing free-floating things." Moreover, it was a time when much was going on outside school. Organized protests were in style at the time, and students often were drawn to important issues beyond the classroom walls.[45] Traditional education in the classroom suffered.

> My teaching ground to a halt in this school. The place descended in those years from smugness to chaos, maybe not unlike many others but with melodramatic New York flourishes. Everything became optional, spearheaded by peace marches which spelled the effective end of attendance requirements. I was legally responsible for students I'd never met. Who in liberal New York dared keep a student from following her conscience and the crowd?[46]

Peck found a small outlet for his frustrations in writing two poems about students, the first of which was published in *Saturday Review* in 1969. Entitled "Nancy," it characterizes a wealthy, smug, but vulnerable female student challenging the teacher, who, in spite of repeated attacks about the irrelevance of his teaching, remains sympathetic. The second poem, "Early Admission," written in 1971 but never published, appears in the poetry chapter later in this book.

During these years he also composed a series of writing activities that were published as part of the *Open Court Correlated Language Arts Program* textbook in 1967.

Having received tenure at Hunter but longing to have a more effective voice in the educational world, Peck applied for and was granted a one-year Harold L. Clapp Fellowship, which gave him the title of assistant director of the Council for Basic Education in Washington, D.C. Expecting it to be a year off, Peck packed his bags. "I thought: I'll go to Washington; I can sit down; I won't have to do lesson plans."

The Council for Basic Education is a small privately funded organization that monitors and evaluates educational innovations. In 1969 they were focusing on English education, and, as Peck puts it:

They decided to give a fellowship to a working classroom teacher who could write. . . . When I got there they said: "The year is yours. If you want to sit around and read educational materials, you may do so. If you want to work up a project, you can do that. If you want to help us with our publications and our monthly newsletter, come on in and do that." And that's what I wanted to do: I wanted to *write*. . . .

I could write an article and take it into the next room, the editor was sitting in there and he'd say, "yes, yes, no, no, change that . . ." and I began to see how to write a newsletter.

And I'd go out and sit in classrooms where I'd never been before— black classrooms for example—and see all kinds of programs.

By the time he returned to the classroom in New York City, he was convinced that he needed to try to be a writer. He taught at Hunter for one more semester and turned in his grade book on 24 May 1971. "You always remember the day you turned in your tenure," he says.

Because of his contacts with publishers, Peck had already published other works in addition to his first essay anthology before he left teaching. The poetry anthology he had been compiling was published in 1970 as *Sounds and Silences: Poetry for Now*. In that collection, among the work of other contemporary poets he included one of his own poems: "The Geese." In 1971, his second poetry anthology, *Mindscapes*, was published. In it he included two more of his own poems: "Mission Uncontrolled" and "Jump Shot." "Jump Shot," about basketball, and "TKO," about boxing, were printed that same year in an anthology titled *Sports Poems*, edited by R. R. Knudson and P. K. Ebert. Another of his poems, "Street Trio," was published in the *Saturday Review* that same year, and two articles about education appeared in magazines addressed to parents: "Can Students Evaluate Their Education?" and "We Can Save Our Schools." He had not yet tried to write fiction, though he says with a straight face that his first fictional work was his attendance book at Hunter.

Had he taught other kinds of students in a different kind of school, Richard Peck might never have become a novelist. He says: "If I had been teaching in the Middlewest where my friends were, I would have ridden out the storm. Had I stayed in the Midwest, I also wouldn't have made personal contact with the publishers . . . and I wouldn't have known what's up."

His teaching career had been filled with disappointments. He saw school curriculums deteriorating, standards collapsing. Parents at home had lost or given up control of their children. Peck recalls noticing one eighth-grade girl who seemed different from the rest, but he didn't know why she seemed different.

> Then one day she fell out into the aisle with a drug overdose. That was my introduction to the drug culture. When we contacted her mother, her mother thought she lived with her grandmother; and when we contacted her grandmother, her grandmother thought she lived with her mother. That was one of the weeks I began to quit.

Peck also recalls one girl who believed she was too gifted to type, another who felt she was so talented that she didn't need to do library research. Teenagers, he concluded, had established "a country of themselves."

But he has never been bitter, has always tried to look beyond the symptoms and the problems. "I tried to see through their defenses to themselves, huddled inside," he says.[47] But it was useless. He had never been able to teach as he remembered being taught. And in the end he says, "It seemed to me that teaching had begun to turn into something that looked weirdly like psychiatric social work—a field in which I was not trained or interested."[48]

Although Richard Peck felt he had not taught his students very much, he knew his students had provided him with almost all of the material he needed to get started as a young adult novelist. First, he had an insider's view of how teenagers behaved, dressed, talked, and interacted as well as what they valued. Second, he had learned what young people like and want in a book: they want to be entertained, and they want to be reassured.

Peck also knew he wasn't writing for all students. It wasn't difficult for him to see that not everyone is a reader. So he aimed his writing at "students who were willing and able to spend a part of their leisure time with books." He explains:

As a teacher, I'd already learned that you can only teach those who are willing to be taught. I'd learned too, that the best, most independent, most promising students were the thoughtful, quiet ones—students who will reach for a book in search of themselves—who often get overlooked in our crisis-oriented society and the schools that mirror it.[49]

And so, he carried his typewriter into the garden of his Brooklyn home and "I began writing a novel to some of the young people I'd left behind in the classroom."[50]

It was a courageous act. Most of the best-known contemporary young adult novelists began writing fiction while they still had support from other jobs. For example, Paula Danziger and Robin Brancato were employed as classroom teachers until their novels sold well enough to enable them to leave their jobs and write full time. Robert Cormier was a newspaper writer and editor when his first novels were published. Other writers—Judy Blume, Norma Klein, Bette Greene among them—have had husbands whose incomes have been able to support them until royalties from their novels made them self-sufficient. But Richard Peck was unmarried, and at the age of thirty-seven gave up his teaching income along with his group medical insurance and his retirement plan, determined to make it as a writer on his own. Even more risky was the fact that he had no experience writing fiction. He told one interviewer: "'When I was doing that first book, I never went out of the house for fear of spending money.'"[51] But it was, he says, the only time in his life that he didn't worry about the future. "I didn't dare. I just thought about *now*. I didn't even worry about what I was going to do to make a living if this didn't work."

Many authors, whether writing fiction for adults or young adults, write from their personal experiences—especially in their first novel. Richard Peck maintains that he has never consciously written anything autobiographical. "My past is my own," he states. "I grew up in an age now grown mythic, an age of debating teams and draft cards and diagrammed sentences and dance programs. It's an old story, and my readers don't believe it."[52] Furthermore, as an examination of his childhood, his education, and his previous comments have made clear, Peck says: "I was always more interested in other people's lives than in mine, right from the beginning." So for his ideas and inspiration he depends on the ideas and experiences of others, especially of kids.

He finished writing his first novel, based in part on experiences his friends Jean and Richard Hughes had had in providing a home for unwed teenage mothers, in a little more than four months. In spite of all he had heard about the difficulty of finding someone to publish one's first novel, Peck neatly piled his manuscript of *Don't Look and It Won't Hurt* into a small box and hand carried it to George Nicholson, then editor-in-chief of juvenile books at Holt, Rinehart & Winston. On the following day Peck's phone rang and George Nicholson said: "You can start your second novel." That first novel sold more than a half million copies during its first ten years in print.[53]

To further support himself during 1972 and 1973 he wrote occasional pieces on travel, local history, and the architecture of historical neighborhoods for the *New York Times*, and published articles in *Saturday Review, House Beautiful,* and *American Libraries,* along with a poem in the *Chicago Tribune.* A book begun earlier with Mortimer Smith and George Weber at the Council for Basic Studies—*A Consumer's Guide to Educational Innovations*—was also released in 1972.

But writing novels for young adults was Peck's main interest. In quick succession he wrote his second and third young adult novels, *Dreamland Lake* and *Through a Brief Darkness,* both published in 1973. In addition, his second collection of essays, entitled *Leap into Reality: Essays for Now,* was published, along with a compilation of articles entitled *Urban Studies: A Research Paper Casebook,* and a variety of writing and teaching activities for *The Creative Word,* vol. 2, with Stephen Judy.

In the next year Peck published his fourth novel, *Representing Super Doll,* along with the scholarly *Transitions: A Literary Paper Casebook* and a series of review columns in *American Libraries*—that journal's first column on young adult books. In succeeding years, Richard Peck has produced a young adult novel each year, with the exception of 1980 when he published his first novel for adults,

Amanda/Miranda. In 1976, along with his best-selling young adult novel, *Are You in the House Alone?*, he produced a third collection of poetry entitled *Pictures That Storm Inside My Head: Poems for the Inner You.* In 1977, along with *Ghosts I Have Been*, he wrote the story for a picture book, illustrated by Don Freeman, called *Monster Night at Grandma's House.* In 1981, after the publication of *Close Enough to Touch*, came a second novel for adults, *New York Time.* And in 1983 he published his epic novel, *This Family of Women*, a book recommended for young adults as well as adults, along with his third Blossom Culp novel, *The Dreadful Future of Blossom Culp.* With the publication of the paperback edition of *Princess Ashley* in October 1988, Dell Publishing Company reports that they alone have printed over three million paperback copies of Richard Peck's novels.[54] An impressive achievement indeed.

2. The Writer

"What is your writing schedule like?" or "What is a typical day for you?" are questions almost everyone asks of writers. Some writers prefer writing early in the morning. A few seem to do their best work late at night. Most try to hold to the routine of a daily schedule. Not Richard Peck, although he does have a routine to start the day:

> These days I get up in the morning; I get dressed; I go out and drink coffee in public, walk around the block, and come back and pretend that I have arrived at my office. One of the great advantages of writing for yourself is that you don't have to commute. But once you're a writer, you go out and pretend to be a commuter. I've heard of weirder routines than that, but . . . We all have our idiosyncrasies and it's all better than alcohol.

His "office" is one room of a modest and very neat New York City apartment on 72nd Street, attractively furnished with antiques from the early 1900s and accentuated by the vibrant red of several small Oriental carpets. A large window with a southern exposure in his workroom provides a ninth-floor view of neighborhood roofs and mostly nondescript buildings—nothing inspiring or distracting. In contrast to the antique furniture, Peck's desk consists of what he describes as "a slab of unhistoric Formica held up at both ends by filing

View from Richard Peck's New York apartment, Dec. 1987.
Photo by Don Gallo.

cabinets." On a metal stand beside his desk sits his old, sturdy, and reliable Royal Standard typewriter, the same one on which he wrote his graduate thesis. As with almost everything else, Richard Peck prefers the comfort and reliability of older things, resisting the trend to computers with word processors. "I don't want anything in the room thinking faster than I," he is quick to explain.

But he does not have a typical daily schedule. When he is at the typewriter, he seems to accomplish more later in the day. "I'm not a morning person," he asserts. "That's the time I answer my mail." By not having to commute, he says he is very productive between 4:30 and 6:30 P.M. when no one else is. And he writes "with a willing appetite the later it gets." "I think that comes from teaching. My idea of night is to go back in there and get ready for tomorrow—which is pretty much what school teachers do."

While most writers purport to prefer isolation, without phone calls, without interruptions of any kind, Peck welcomes them as a respite from the solitude of writing. In the beginning of his literary career the hardest part of writing for a living, Peck asserts, wasn't the uncertainty of it. It was the isolation. "I was used to being surrounded by students and other teachers from dawn on. Life had been divided into segments by ringing bells and interrupted by fire drills. I was used to being besieged by voices, activity." Now, he jokes straight-faced, "I pay people to call me up."

Richard Peck is likely to start slowly on a new novel, but the further he gets into it, the longer he will work on it. "I *gather* enthusiasm as I write." Then he doesn't want the phone to ring. At that point in the creative process, he says, "my own life has no meaning; I'm in the world of my book. I just wish I could move that up to the beginning of the novel."

Although he is away from home nearly one-fourth of the time, he is unable to write while on the road. "I'd be terribly distracted if I tried to write when I'm outside New York." Ironically, Peck finds no distractions living in one of the busiest and most exciting cities in the world. "I've lived in New York long enough not to have any place to go," he explains.

While there is no consistent pattern to his days, there is a pattern to the way Peck goes about starting, developing, and revising a novel. He starts with theme. "Again, that's the school teacher's view: What is the story trying to divulge? . . . Not what's the story about, but why was it written?" His ideas for themes come from a variety of sources, though none of them directly from his own personal experiences. Many of those ideas come from teenagers themselves.

For example, his satire *Secrets of the Shopping Mall* was the result of comments young people made in their letters to him about how much time they spend in local shopping centers after school . . . or instead of going to school. He wrote *Remembering the Good Times* because he had heard about a seventh-grade boy who had told twelve of his classmates that he was going to kill himself; they did nothing about it, but the boy did what he promised. And it was junior high school readers who kept asking Peck when he was going to write a story about the supernatural. "They wanted WEIRD while I was trying to be understanding of their problems."

Spurred by their interest, he wrote *The Ghost Belonged to Me*, with Alexander Armsworth as the main character and the ghost of a dead girl who haunts the loft of a barn. "I would never have thought of a ghost story," Peck admits. "And I never had more fun in my life."[1] "I try to write what young people ask for," he says, "but I don't give them *everything* they want. I don't want to tell them that marrying means living happily ever after. I don't want to tell them that there is justice in the world and all you have to do is be nice. It's a compromise ... between what I want and am able to say and what they are willing to read."[2]

In addition, as Peck realized part-way through is career, "At your typewriter you're aging every minute while, mysteriously, your readers remain the same age. Worse yet, they change their protective coloring, their fads in clothes and speech and music, every semester. And they live different lives in different parts of the country."[3] What, Peck asked himself, is the best way to find out about those elements of real-life teenagers?

> You can't ask the kids' parents, because the parents have lost contact with them at the age of twelve, and I need to know what happens to them *after* the age of twelve. You can't find out much from their teachers, because the school day is so short and the teachers have so little authority over the students. You really have to go to the kids themselves.[4]

So, early in his writing career Richard Peck started a habit of leaving his typewriter to travel across the country, speaking in up to sixty schools and libraries a year, talking with teachers and librarians, and, most of all, meeting with kids. He has talked with young people in wealthy Connecticut suburban junior high schools and in poor inner-city high schools in Cleveland; he's discussed his books with rural students in a sheep station high in the Colorado Rockies and on a raft in a logging community in Ketchikan, Alaska. In addition, he thrives on the letters he receives from readers. From these students he gets reassurance for what he has written and ideas for what he still needs to write. "I've come to count on every new generation of the young for book ideas better than mine," he admits in "Coming Full Circle."[5]

His most helpful source of information for *Princess Ashley* was the daughter of his friends in Illinois who provided him with the background for his first novel. "I wanted the setting of the novel to be an absolutely real American high school, not my version or my vision, but the way it *is*." And so he went to Courtney Hughes, who was at that time a senior in New Trier High School in Winnetka, Illinois.

> Being a senior, she really knew her way around that school. Also she was on her way out—she would graduate before the book came out. When I needed something I could call her up and say, "What do you call this? . . . What happens in the school if this situation comes up?" She's very verbal and she told me about high school life. And she did something else that helped more than anything else: every time the high school newspaper came out, she sent me a copy. So I knew what was really important to those students at that time.[6]

Although he looks for real-life situations, Richard Peck does not look for real-life models for his characters:

> Real people are never enough, and real people never do what you want them to do in the novel. But you can take a bit—even a piece of clothing, for example. I don't want to get too caught up in that [kind of detail], but I want my characters to be dressed the way my readers are. "Well," you say, "what about ten years from now when styles have changed?" You can't think about that, you have to make a stand, and I don't think it matters. . . . Years ago I put Guess? jeans in a novel because I heard about them at some snooty school, and sure enough, they're still around. I got lucky.[7]

The luckiest thing Peck ever did, he says, was when he was writing *Are You in the House Alone* in 1975:

> I knew nothing about music at the time—*nothing*. But I needed a popular singer that the girl liked and was listening to—just the name of a singer. And, blindly, I reached out and I took the first singer whose name I saw in an article. Bruce Springsteen. I had never heard of him, but I put him in. His career fizzled a year later; I never thought of him again. Eight years later he was the biggest thing in show business and it makes my novel look much newer than it is. I'll never be that lucky again.[8]

Although such minute triumphs aren't vital to a novel's success, Peck feels they are important for his morale. "They keep me looking," he says, "they keep me sharpening my eye. They make me say, 'Why is she doing that? Why has she drilled three holes in one ear instead of just one?' "[9]

Peck especially values the input he gets from young people who live in suburbs. Having grown up in a small town with strong rural connections and having lived most of his adult life in New York City, Peck says of suburbs: "That's not a life that attracts me, or that I know very well. So I have to go and find out about it." Fortunately for Richard Peck, young people have been willing to talk about their lives and experiences.

"But even without this help," he adds, "the truth is I'd rather be in the classroom than anywhere else, trying to see through the surface changes to the old, eternal questions hanging unasked in the room: Am I cool enough? Will I ever be loved? If they really knew who I was, would I be forgiven?"[10]

Once he has the theme in mind, Peck searches for an effective spokesperson for the book.

> I know it has to be young. In my first novel [*Don't Look and It Won't Hurt*], I went through three. I thought the unwed mother had a right to tell her own story; she couldn't—she was too self-delusive. Then I thought her younger brother would be the right distance; he wasn't—he was a boy who couldn't handle his emotions. Then I came up with a younger sister who hadn't gotten herself into trouble and therefore looked at her older sister with a critical eye, and that gave the cutting edge to the novel.

In *Are You in the House Alone?* Peck felt that only the victim could tell the story, and she did. But when he began *Remembering the Good Times* in the voice of the eventual suicide victim, it didn't work. If Travis had been able to express himself and explain what was happening to him, he probably wouldn't have had to kill himself. The story was better told, Peck discovered, by a friend—a boy friend rather than a girl friend.

When he started writing fiction, Peck discovered that if he wrote in third-person omniscient, "I was speaking as an adult, and I sounded like a teacher conducting a class," he told interviewer Jean W. Ross.[11] And so he almost always writes in the voice of a teenager. "I think readers are looking for someone to talk to—so I start with the . . . human voice."[12] Among his fifteen novels for young adults, only *Through a Brief Darkness* and *Secrets of the Shopping Mall* are written in third-person, author omniscient voice.

Writing dialogue is Peck's favorite part of constructing a novel. He attributes that to his interest in listening to people, going back to his Illinois childhood where he eavesdropped on the conversations of all those relatives. "When I'm coming to a scene of conversation, then I feel as if I'm going to a party." But he doesn't feel comfortable creating the dialogue out of his own imagination. And so, he says, "I carry a note pad. I sit behind people in buses and listen in shopping areas and take dialogue down. I can't think up a lot of that dialogue: I've got to use the language I hear."[13]

From theme and characterization, Peck moves to setting next, in the same way an English teacher might lead his students through an examination of a novel. He asks: "What does this novel tell about the life of its time? Very few people ask that question about a novel, but teachers *do*."

Peck's settings, except for his earliest young adult novels or those in historical locales, are always somewhere in suburbia, because, he says, "that's where my readers live." He feels comfortable with setting "because I am a Midwesterner," he says, "and we are born with compasses in our heads and long distances and we can tell the differences in terrain."

Researching the setting, the dialogue, and the various aspects of contemporary teenage life is one of the most pleasurable activities for Richard Peck. In addition to serving as a primer for his pump, as he has put it,[14] it's a process he has felt comfortable with since his university days. "Nobody ever taught me how to write a novel," he declares, "but I was trained by graduate school professors to do research; to take notes and to be able to read them later; to draw upon the world." Then he adds with a smile in his voice: "I even know how to use the library."[15]

After that he is ready to develop the plot:

The day comes when you have to call a halt to your research and go home to sit before a mute typewriter until you begin to hear voices in the room. Voices that never were. Young voices, but a little wiser, a little less self-delusive than the young.

When those voices become coherent and then insistent, you begin to type. More of the creative process than that I do not know.[16]

But plot intimidates him, he admits. "I don't like plot. I don't read for plot. And I think a novel that is overplotted is weak." His approach is to start somewhere and see where it goes:

There are some elements of the plot that I just can't foresee; I couldn't outline the book. I try sometimes but I don't get very far. And I realize now that I *don't* want to do that: it would put [the characters] in a straightjacket; it would also make them marionettes, dancing to my tune. A lot happens in a novel that I didn't perceive. . . . It's the unexpected event that has to be woven in seamlessly as if you saw it coming the day you started writing the novel.

In developing his stories, Richard Peck never rushes through an entire first draft just to get the basic story down before he goes back to rework it. He starts with the opening scene and develops the novel scene by consecutive scene. "I never jump ahead. Some people write the ending and then write up to it, and I see the virtue of that, but the ending is full of stuff I don't know about! So I couldn't do it." He writes an average of seven drafts, although the earlier chapters in the developing novel are rewritten far more times, the first chapter as many as twenty-five times, Peck estimates. Catching his breath after the completion of his latest novel, he regrets rewriting the beginning so many times. "I should just *leave* the first chapter after six or seven tries, go on, and then come back at the end. But, oh no, if I don't go back over every word of the first chapter I can't figure out how the rest goes."

Unlike some writers who share their works in progress with a close friend, trusted colleague, or sympathetic editor, no one sees Richard Peck's latest novel until he is satisfied with it and it is ready for his editor's evaluation. The only exception is when he occasionally reads a specific scene to a small group of students and asks them what they think will happen next.

Although Peck delivers his completed manuscript to his editor with the false assumption that it is ready for printing, he is always grateful for the editor's viewpoint, especially when that editor finds something the writer has missed. "You think you've got that scene there and you go back and look at it and you say, 'Oh, that scene: I wrote it in my head, I didn't write it on the paper.' And that's useful." But he does not want to share the creative process of developing the novel with an editor. "I want to give the editor as finished a product as possible so we can get down to smaller fine points and not big concepts. . . . I want to do all the editing within a month and get on to production."

After the book is released, there are the reviews to deal with—an uneasy period for Peck. "That's one more group of adults you have to work through," he says with just a little pique in his voice. Even though most of the reviews of his novels have been very positive, he exhibits that insecure feeling most writers—and probably all creative artists—seem to have when their latest creation is unveiled. He explains:

> I don't want to get caught up in reviews. I don't want a good review to please me because I wasn't writing for the reviewer—he didn't pay for the book, and he's the wrong age, and he's reading too many books. And I don't want a bad review to make me mad. Besides, my readers don't read reviews. . . . I save the reviews but I don't look at them again or think much about them.

The most important responses come from young readers. Letters from teenagers provide Peck with ideas for future books as well as let him know what worked best in his previous novels. Although he keeps no record of the number of letters he gets in a typical week, he does notice patterns during the year. The best letters, he says, come in the summer, "because they're self-solicited." It's easy to notice when teachers have assigned students to write a letter to an author. "Most teachers are so glad to see students write anything, that they will not only grade their rough drafts, they'll mail them! In fact, I will get letters that are marked by the teacher." He answers all of the letters that he can decipher, he says, giving more thoughtful responses to those he receives in the summer "because they're not coming in droves."

Whichever way and at whatever time they come, those letters complete the process of creation that Peck began as much as two or more years earlier. And the responses and ideas they contain help regenerate the process as Peck searches for new ideas for the theme of his next book and listens for clues to the language and interests of today's young readers.

3. The Teacher

Although Richard Peck left the profession of teaching in 1971, his appetite for teaching has never left him. "I am an old school teacher," he admits, "and I do want to give lessons."[1] As a break from the discipline of writing, Peck has taught courses in young adult literature through Louisiana State University's School of Graduate Librarianship with Dr. Patsy Perritt, on the main campus in Baton Rouge and in Shreveport, as well as in a special summer study program in England. In addition, he has been a lecturer and teacher of creative writing on cruise ships to Europe, an activity that provided him with the background for his most recent novel, *Those Summer Girls I Never Met.*

Watching him speak to a group—whether of students or adults —an observer gets the impression that teaching comes naturally to Peck. In any presentation he makes, he is always well prepared with specific ideas and helpful advice, but he is also fast and sharp with responses to questions. His statements are pointed if not barbed. He tells listeners:

- *A*'s are the end of education. Nobody learns from an *A*.

- Watching television is what you do with your life when you don't want to live it.

- Writing is not self-expression; writing is communication. Nobody wants to read your diary except your mother.

- Puberty is deciding at the age of twelve or so to divorce your own parents, charging irreconcilable differences.

- While puberty is the death of childhood, it isn't the birth of reason.

- If there's anything the young despise it's *novelty.* That's one reason their social life is so monotonous. And why they will cut school to keep abreast of daytime soap operas.[2]

A newspaper reporter in Alaska wrote that "Richard Peck rattles off streaks of wisdom like a barrage of Northern Lights."[3] A writer in Indiana observed that, when talking with students, Peck " strangles their ideals with a satin sash. A gentle charm helps soften his attacks on the extended adolescent, the unimaginative or just plain uninteresting kid."[4] If the audience is slow to respond, Peck uses some old and effective teaching methods for involving the group: posing questions, calling on individuals for their opinions, asking for a raise of hands.

No matter what his approach, Richard Peck enjoys performing before a group. In fact, he would rather speak than write. Writing is hard, frustrating, lonely. "I feel more myself in giving a speech," he acknowledges. "Making a speech is the only place in my life I've found where I didn't know about the past and the future—it's just now. . . . You get immediate response. The deadline is already there . . . oh, yes. Speaking is the reward for having written."

Observe Peck in front of a gathering of about three dozen students and a few adults—teachers and librarians, and a parent or two—on an unusually warm December afternoon in 1987. The room in the Montclair, New Jersey, Public Library is overheated and growing warmer. Richard Peck talks about himself, since that is part of what he was invited here to do. But he wants students to participate, and so from time to time he asks them fill-in-the-blank questions that are open-ended:

The most important thing you can give your friend is⎯⎯⎯⎯⎯⎯.

Every poet needs to be ⎯⎯⎯⎯⎯⎯.

Or he presents a situation that occurs at the start of one of his novels and asks the audience what they think will happen next. There is a "right" answer, of course, because the inquirer is leading into an issue he has already addressed in one of his novels. But Peck doesn't let off-target answers escape him; the students' responses reveal what's important to them, and Peck is likely to store those in his mind (and possibly later in his notes) for future reference. He also never tells a student that his or her answer is wrong. He may give the respondent a quizzical look or a crooked smile, but he doesn't want to inhibit additional responses.

A second purpose today is to respond to students in the audience who, through their teachers, sent him poems and stories they had written weeks before. Although he felt some resentment at having had to read so many papers (about eighty of them), he diligently wrote comments on every one. In addition, he copied some of the best verses and descriptive paragraphs on a sheet of paper, had that duplicated, and has distributed copies to everyone in attendance as examples of the best writing. Throughout the afternoon session he continually refers to those examples, while also noting elements of his own writing, teaching the audience what good writing is and suggesting ways to help the students develop their own ideas. Praise is foremost in his comments about the students' work. But he does not allow students to settle for today's accomplishments. "You are all good writers," he says, "and you can all be better."

As he moves through his presentation—which contains comments he has made hundreds of times before, along with statements and stories chosen specifically for this day's audience—he continues to give advice to young writers: "The one voice your story never needs is yours." "If you want to be a writer, you need to read three books a week. You need to see how other people do it. You need to see what the publishers are accepting."[5] In other speeches as well as in articles he has written, he recommends that students study Latin and also learn five new words every week.

In another place at another time, he has advice for parents about motivating their children to read:

> Never imply by word or attitude that reading and writing are "woman's work." . . .
> Never worry about a book corrupting a child. And never blame a book for having given sex education you haven't gotten around to. Worry if your children are not getting ideas from books. . . .
> Never use a book as a scapegoat for an inability to control the child's television addiction. . . .
> Read aloud to kids as much as possible, and don't stop even after they can read for themselves. . . .
> Make sure there are maps in the house. Maps remind the young that they aren't the center of the universe. . . .
> Let kids observe adults who read books, magazines and newspapers that reflect various tastes and interests. Independent reading is the badge of adulthood, and the young are hungry for the advantages of maturity.[6]

To English teachers he explains what he tries to do in his novels:

> Today I'm still trying to hold the attention of the young, to deal with a diminished attention span, to explore subject matter of immediate and manifest relevance, to vie with the distractions of television and peer-group pressure and the disarray of permissive home lives. I don't suggest that my novels are didactic—or dare to be. We live in an age and country in which we approach our young by indirection.[7]

In his recent speeches to teachers, he recommends books for them to teach, approaching from the stance that these are books he would teach if he were teaching today. His suggestions vary as new novels come to his attention, but first on his list is always Robert Cormier's *The Chocolate War*. "That's a novel that will be read in a hundred years. . . . I wouldn't let anyone get through high school without reading that book because it's on one of the most important issues today—that is, what happens when power shifts to the young, away from adults."[8] In his most recent speeches his next recommendation is M.E. Kerr's *Night Kites*, "because of its structure," not just because it deals with the timely topic of AIDS. Third is Chris

Crutcher's *Running Loose*, "because it's one book on the subject of what are we going to do about a school that is run by the coach not the principal." He adds, "When I read [that book] I'm high for a week. Look what somebody did in this field!"

He also has provided English and reading teachers with "Ten Questions to Ask about a Novel." They include: "What would this story be like if the main character were of the opposite sex?" "Why is this story set where it is (not *what* is the setting)?" "How is the main character different from you?" "Reread the first paragraph of Chapter 1. What's in it that makes you read on?"[9]

With young adult librarians, Peck feels his greatest affinity, because, as he tells a convention gathering of them: "In the 1980s we writers and librarians have come into our own. We are the people left willing to know the young. Everyone else in their lives has recoiled from them and is still looking for ways to abdicate authority." Together, Peck believes that writers and librarians can reach some young people through compromise. "We always dealt in a product and a service that only a minority cared about," he adds.[10]

For his captivated audience he defines adolescence as he sees it: "Adolescence is the gnawing need to lose your innocence while retaining your illusions." He tells them some "truths" he'd like to tell teenagers, though he knows kids wouldn't listen. Among those "truths" are: "[A]ll mass movements . . . are designed to keep you down"; "[P]eople rise individually if at all"; "[L]ove may be eternal, but romance has a time limit"; "[I]n youth, laughter is a weapon, but in maturity it's a cure"; "[Y]ou will be held responsible for the consequences of your actions."[11]

To succeed with teenagers, writers and librarians must be crafty. "Our job seems to be," he says,

- to plant a challenge in a novel that looks reassuring.
- to put a new book behind cover art that looks comfortably cliched.
- to bootleg inspiration in a format of escape.[12]

To help kids through adolescence, Peck concludes, "Only books help. Only books let you down easy as fiction nudges you a little nearer fact, as you stand in the shoes of a book character and test yourself."[13]

For both librarians and interested teachers, Richard Peck—who travels probably more than almost any other young adult author— provides some solid advice to follow when inviting an author to speak. In "Care and Feeding of the Visiting Author," he explains all the important things to do: contacting authors (through publishers); limiting the size of the group; preparing the students and teachers for the speaker's presentation; ordering copies of books; arranging to pick up, transport, house, and feed the author; and paying the honoraria.[14] It's helpful information, from an expert.

One day early in 1986 Richard Peck was searching for an ending to a speech that would be both instructive and entertaining. In desperation, he claims that he thought "Help me God." Inspiration came to him in an instant: a prayer! So he wrote "A Teenager's Prayer" to end that speech. It later appeared in print in the September–October 1986 issue of *Horn Book*.[15] Since then, Peck says, "I think that 'Teenager's Prayer' has probably been read by far more people than ever read a novel of mine!" He later followed that prayer with "The Fervent Prayer of a Teenager's Parent," which appeared in the Winter 1987 issue of *The ALAN Review*[16] as well as other places, and more recently by "A Teacher's Prayer," which first appeared as part of a publicity flyer from Dell Publishing Company advertising *Princess Ashley*.[17] Here, with Richard Peck's blessing, are all three prayers, for the first time in one place:

A Teenager's Prayer

Oh Supreme Being, and I don't mean me:
Give me the vision to see my parents as human beings
because if they aren't, what does that make me?
Give me vocabulary because the more I say *you know*,
the less anyone does.
Give me freedom from television because I'm beginning
to suspect its happy endings.
Give me sex education to correct what I first heard
from thirteen-year-olds.
Give me homework to keep me from flunking Free Time.
Give me a map of the world so I may see that this town

and I are not the center of it.
Give me the knowledge that conformity is the enemy of
friendship.
Give me the understanding that nobody ever grows up in a
group so I may find my own way.
Give me limits so I will know I am loved.
And give me nothing I haven't earned so that this adolescence
will not last forever.

Amen

The Fervent Prayer of a Teenager's Parent

Oh Higher Power,
And I wish I were—
Give me to know that the easier life is made for the young, the harder they
will make it for themselves and each other.
Harden my heart and stop my ears against what Other People let THEIR
kids do.
Strike me dumb when I blame a teacher I have never met, for heaven alone
knows what that teacher has heard about me.
Let not the coach build his career on the vulnerable flesh of my son.
Spare my daughter the sly pornography of soap operas.
Send summer reading lists so my children won't lose three months of a fer-
tile growing season.
Sharpen my eye as I ransack my child's room to find and destroy the
fake I.D.
Embolden my heart as I unplug the telephone from my child's room so
that the peer group that rules the school all day will not rule our nights
as well.
Stay my hand when I am tempted to buy my children's love with credit
cards in their names, or mine.
Strengthen my spine as I impose a curfew, lest my nights be a hell of waiting for the fatal phone call.
And give me ears to hear that when the young cry out for new freedoms,
they are demanding old rules.

Amen

A Teacher's Prayer

OH GOD, I'M ONLY A TEACHER,
and it's lonely work because I'm the only member of my species in the room.
I like kids, and I love my subject matter,
and I have higher hopes for these kids of mine than they have for themselves:
I want them to create. They want to consume.

I want them to love the world. They want the world to love them.
I want every day to be different. They want every day to be the same.
I want them to burn with zeal, about something. They want to be cool, about everything.
I want them to think. They want me to tell them.
I want the bell to ring. They want the bell to ring.

OH GOD, I'M A TEACHER,

I'm not their buddy, I don't want to be. I've seen what they do to their buddies.
I'm not their parent, and yet they're looking high and low for parents and can't seem to find them.
I'm their teacher. I don't want them to take me at my word.
I want them to find the words.

OH GOD, I'M A TEACHER,

So I'm perfectly willing to move mountains. If you'll send me some hands for my end of the lever:
Send me a couple of administrators who care more about standards than they do about their jobs.
Send me an occasional parent who sees in me a colleague, not a scapegoat.
Send me a few kids every year, willing to brave their peers in order to learn.

OH GOD, I'M ONLY A TEACHER,

I want to make bricks. Could you send me some straw?

AMEN

4. Essays and Essay Collections

Although he is best known as a young adult novelist, Richard Peck began his writing career by publishing nonfiction. His essays have appeared in professional journals such as *School Library Journal*, in popular magazines such as *Parents' Magazine* and *Better Family Living*, and in newspapers such as the *New York Times*, along with book reviews in the *Los Angeles Times* and in *American Libraries*. While those articles deal mostly with books and writing for teenagers, several of them also deal with antiques, architecture, and travel. He has also written educational materials for textbooks and compiled and edited two collections of essays for high school students.

His first piece was the self-published *Old Town, A Complete Guide*. Then his writing experiences while a fellow with the Council for Basic Education provided him with additional opportunities to see his words in print in monthly newsletters as well as in publications such as *A Consumer's Guide to Educational Innovations*.

But the work that Peck sees as his initiation into the world of major commercial publishing resulted from his association with the late Ned Hoopes at Hunter College High School. As Peck tells it: "Here I was, new in New York, and he came up to me at the first faculty meeting and said 'Let's do a book.'" This was the mid-1960s and Richard Peck knew he had to do more than just lecture and assign readings from traditional anthologies in order to reach his New York City students. When asked what kind of book he would like to do, the young teacher replied: "Well, I will need a collection of non-fiction, contemporary readings for my students that they cannot reject as irrelevant." The result was *Edge of Awareness: Twenty-Five Contemporary Essays.* The title page says "Edited by Ned E. Hoopes and Richard Peck," but it was Peck who did most of the legwork to put the book together. Hoopes knew what would sell and he had the contacts with publishers. In November 1966 Dell published the collection in paperback. "It sold *millions* of copies," says Peck. What a way to start! And it has remained in print ever since.

Divided into five sections, under such headings as "Searching for Meaning in a Complex Society" and "Surviving through Science," the twenty-five essays in *Edge of Awareness* provide mature and thought-provoking perspectives on contemporary society. Readers will find the thoughts of twentieth-century historians, scientists, anthropologists, and statesmen such as Arnold Toynbee, Margaret Mead, and Adlai E. Stevenson among those of poets and other creative artists such as E.M. Forster, Lillian Ross, and John Ciardi reprinted from prestigious publications such as *The New Yorker, Saturday Review,* and the *New York Times* and various books of importance during that time period.

Seven years later, just as Richard Peck was publishing his first novels for teenagers, Dell released Peck's second collection of contemporary essays. Entitled *Leap into Reality: Essays for Now,* this anthology contains thirty pieces, most of which first appeared in the late 1960s in such magazines as *Harper's, The American Scholar, Smithsonian, Esquire,* and *Newsweek,* as well as the *New York Times.* Authorities such as historian Barbara Tuchman, microbiologist René Dubois, anthropologist Loren Eiseley, composer Leonard Bernstein, educator Jonathan Kozol, and writer James Baldwin provide a veritable *Who's Who* of cultural literacy of the sixties. These pieces are, as Peck notes in his introduction, ingredients in a time capsule that provide, for future readers, an indication of what was important to significant writers of the late sixties and early seventies.[1]

Although these two collections are noteworthy for what they contain, they have two weaknesses. In spite of the effort to reflect the spirit and the key issues of the times, only three of the essays in each of the collections are written by women. It must be noted also that the adult perspectives and the highly sophisticated quality of the writing make these collections difficult reading fare for all but the most advanced high school students. In fact, although Peck intended these books to be used in tenth grade, the majority of their sales are now to college classes.

In the early seventies, after he had just left teaching to try to "make it" as a professional writer, Richard Peck wrote a variety of articles on antiques, architecture, history, and travel. For the *New York Times* he wrote occasional pieces about the architecture of historic neighborhoods in New York City. In both *Saturday Review* and *House Beautiful* he wrote about Art Deco—from bracelets and pendants to the walls and tower of the Chrysler Building.

Nostalgia, a trademark of many of Peck's novels for both teenagers and adults, is evident in his travel as well as his antique pieces—for example, in his description of the mix of past and present on Governors Island[2] or in a *New York Times* article about the last trolley running in New Orleans: the St. Charles.[3]

To learn about the field of books he was entering in the early 1970s, Peck read the competition extensively. His acquaintance with the growing field of young adult books as well as with publishers gave him an entrance into more than one part of the publishing world, and he was asked to write a quarterly series of book reviews for the "Current" column in *American Libraries* starting in February 1974. It was that publication's first column on young adult books.

In the five columns he wrote, Peck reviewed books with the intent of making "inveterate, habitual, chronic readers out of the citizens of the 21st century."[4] Among other evaluative remarks, he cautioned readers about the roles of irresponsible parents in Isabelle Holland's *Heads You Win, Tails I Lose*, commended Leon Garfield's *The Sound of Chariots*, heaped high praise on the quality of Katie Letcher Lyle's *I Will Go Barefoot All Summer for You* and *Fair Day, and Another Step Begun*, applauded Eve Merriam's collection of autobiographical sketches entitled *Growing Up Female in America: Ten Lives*, criticized the blemishes but extolled the intentions of Sandra Scoppettone's

Trying Hard to Hear You, and introduced readers to the most contro-
versial book of 1974: Robert Cormier's *The Chocolate War,* calling it
"the most uncompromising novel ever directed to the '12 and up
reader'—and very likely the most necessary."⁵ His reviews are fair,
balanced, insightful, and lively, and new ones continue to appear occasionally in the *Los Angeles Times.*

Peck's most incendiary writing occurs in his essays about teaching
and the roles of adults versus young people. The issue of who's-in-
control is the focus of two articles published in magazines for parents
in 1971, the year Peck resigned from teaching at Hunter College
High School. In "We Can Save Our Schools," Peck begins by attack-
ing "naive" educational reformers of the 1960s who had advocated "a
utopian freedom in the classroom where self-directed youngsters
pursue their own interests and learn happily at their own pace."
What resulted, Peck declares, is "a gangland atmosphere in which
the potential achiever is bullied into mediocrity by the non-achiever,
and no one can hear himself think."⁶ In both homes and schools, per-
missiveness and efforts to be "relevant," Peck asserts, "have led to a
sort of torpor and aimlessness among the young."⁷

In "Can Students Evaluate Their Education?" Peck laments the
loss of teacher control: "Young people have lost a guiding hand, but
they have found a loud voice." He sees life in schools as bleak: with
restless, unmotivated students who conform to the empty words of
rebellious leaders; a haphazard curriculum; and crumbled standards.
Parents and teachers, he declares, must encourage in our young people "a renewed respect for documentation—for logic, reason, and
proof—rather than encouraging them to accept glib opinions and
catch phrases."⁹ "Without adults around to set standards, and to put
up a good fight for maintaining them," writes Richard Peck, "young
people fall prey to the confusion that arises when there is no yard-
stick by which to measure achievements and contributions."¹⁰

Those themes—the need for adult authority and the inability of
contemporary teenagers to form a community for each other—are
repeated throughout many of Peck's other published essays, as well
as in his speeches to teachers and librarians. At their strongest, they
are hyperbolic put-downs of kids. Witness these statements from
"People of the World: A Look at Today's Young Adults and Their

Needs," a speech Peck presented to the American Library Association at their 1981 conference in San Francisco and that was printed in *School Library Media Quarterly* that fall:

> When you speak to parents, all their children are gifted. When you speak to the children, they're all remedial.[11]

> Adolescents would prefer to communicate with one another, but they can't because they don't have the vocabulary. They are verbally anorectic and happy to be.[12]

> Most adolescents cannot read well enough today to understand and be entertained by printed matter.[13]

Or this paragraph about teenagers from a guest column Peck wrote in 1985 for *School Library Journal*:

> Wherever they live, they regularly confuse the word for the deed, preaching tolerance and practicing exclusion. They are devoted, undependable friends to one another. They believe group identity will solve personal problems. They refuse to accept the consequences of their own actions, and they can project blame any distance. They believe passionately in surfaces: masks, uniforms, poses, and yet when you pierce their defenses, they seem relieved to see you.[14]

These are some of the key factors that seem to inspire and drive Richard Peck to write novels for teenagers. If young people are misdirected, his novels might set a few of them straight. If teenagers have a confused view of the world, his novels can provide at least one clear alternative view. If kids are, as Peck believes, essentially humorless, he will work extra hard to get humor into his novels. If students are attracted so much to television because it is entertaining, he will attract them to books with what is entertaining to students: "to characters they can befriend, characters they can become."[15] If adults in the real world do not provide adequate, authoritative guidance for young people, then adults in his novels— grandparent figures as well as supportive parents—can. Because there seem to be so few models or opportunities for young adults to grow independently in today's society, he can create characters who choose independence over conformity in books that "invite them to champion themselves, road maps pointing the way out of the subdivision."[16]

Peck describes in most of his articles how he attempts to meet those perceived needs through his novels or how others have done so in their books. In "In the Country of Teenage Fiction" published in 1973, for example, Peck praises Hinton's *The Outsiders*, Kerr's *Dinky Hocker Shoots Smack!*, Stolz's *Leap before You Look*, Richard's *Pistol*, and Campbell's *No More Trains to Tottenville*.[17] In "The Invention of Adolescence and Other Thoughts on Youth" published in 1983, he uses as examples his own *The Ghost Belonged to Me*, *Father Figure*, *Are You in the House Alone?*, and *Close Enough to Touch*.[18] And in "YA Books in the Decade of the Vanishing Adult," he notes examples from Jane O'Connor's *Just Good Friends* and Chris Crutcher's *Running Loose* as well as from his own *Are You in the House Alone?* and *Remembering the Good Times*.[19]

Not all of Peck's essays focus on the failures of today's educational system or the inadequacies of today's young people. Several of his articles focus on an analysis of the elements of good young adult fiction. "Some Thoughts on Adolescent Literature," for example, analyzes three key characteristics of the young adult novel,[20] while "Ten Questions to Ask about a Novel" presents exactly that.[21] The title of "The Care and Feeding of the Visiting Author" is also self-explanatory.[22] And in "The Genteel Unshelving of a Book," Peck recounts a censorship effort that banned his *Father Figure* from a junior high school library because one mother feared that the book would undermine the standards of behavior that she had established for her daughter[23]—an ironic twist on Peck's preoccupation with the lack of parental authority in contemporary society.

5. Poems and Poetry Collections

"Though I believe in poetry and I write poetry, I am not a poet," asserts Richard Peck. Maybe. Consider his accomplishments:

- Although the bulk of his writing is fiction and he has never published enough poetry to comprise even one collection of his own poems, some people who consider themselves to be poets would covet being published in the magazines in which his poems have appeared, most notably *Saturday Review* and the *Chicago Tribune Magazine*.

- He has compiled and edited three anthologies of poems intended for use by junior and senior high school students, the first of which became one of the most widely used collections of contemporary poetry in the 1970s.

- He has managed to include a poem or verse of some sort in almost every novel he has published.

If Richard Peck is not a poet, he certainly has made significant contributions to involve teenagers with the genre. (It is interesting to note that no biographical source on this author has ever made any comments about his poetry.)

Saturday Review published "Nancy," one of his first poems, in 1969 and followed it with others, including "Street Trio" in 1971. In "Street Trio," Peck wryly observes the dress and decorations of a then contemporary couple with their baby on a city street: "She of the electric hair" and "Vampira eyelids," wearing "floral-embroidered Levis" and "Marxist workshirt"; "He of the tie-dyed tank-top," "beaded headband," "rimless glasses," and a "bandito mustachio"; with their baby "Swinging low beneath her liberated bosom / In a denim sling." You can almost see the author smiling as he writes those descriptions and ends with a twist, as lugging the baby along with "a bag of macrobiotic groceries" she staggers behind him into the subway.[1]

"Nancy" exemplifies much of what the author was concerned with then and is still concerned about today: spoiled teenagers vying with adults. Nancy is the sullen, defiant student of the 1960s, wearing an expensive skirt over leather boots, "Trying hard to look hard," threatening anarchy, "burning / With borrowed fire," explaining to the teacher how irrelevant he has been: "Wanting me only to know that I have failed you, / Have driven you to the barricades."[2] The teacher in the poem—mirroring the teacher in the poet—is angered by this kind of overindulged student, is frustrated by the lack of communication between them. Such anger and frustration have been evident in Peck's other works. But as in those other works, beneath that anger and frustration lies a deep concern for the youth behind the appearance.

Those characteristics are reflected in an unpublished poem that Peck wrote in 1971 but that appears in print here for the first time. Through the teacher's "letter" to his student, we see his playful recounting of Mercedes' qualities: her "peer-group leadership potential," her dazzling smile, and her promise. Not mentioned in this recommendation, of course, is anything about her ability as a *student*! Richard Peck says that both of these poems very much reflect the mood he was in during his last semester of teaching. "In fact," he adds, "they are more literal portraits of real students than I would allow myself (or be able to see) today. . . . I loved both those girls; otherwise I could have let them go without poems."

Early Admission

Dear Mercedes:
Need you ask?
Of course I will commend you
To the College of Your Choice.

I'll speak in tongues
Of your verbal expression,
Your peer-group leadership potential,
Your life-adjustment, your promise,
Above all, your promise.

And never breathe a word that
No cloister will contain
Your irrepressible witchery:
That dazzle of smile and eyes
Destined to dissolve deans,
Conquer Graduate Assistants,
Return the oldest dodderer
In Faculty Lounge
To the young buck he never was.

The flirt of your skirt
Through College Hall?
No, I can't quite see
Your bright plumage in all
That gray matter;

Nevertheless, Mercedes,
I'll fill out the form
With Superlatives:
I'll recommend you
To the world.

Not all his poems on serious subjects are so wry. "Jump Shot," first published in *Mindscapes: Poems for the Real World*, vividly details the movements of a basketball player on a city street. With "Hands like stars" spread across the surface of the ball and "Elbows . . . meant for eyesockets," he makes the calculated "arch-back leap" and sends the ball towards the hoop.[3] In "TKO," the poet describes the state of the once-grand Stillman's gym that is now "mostly on the ropes"—no

Kid going twenty-eight rounds, no Irene Dunne watching at ringside—because "They pretty much threw in the towel."[4] Both of those poems are included in an anthology called *Sports Poems*, edited by R. R. Knudson and P. K. Ebert.

Although all of the aforementioned poems are written in free verse, not all of Peck's poems are. "The Geese," a twelve-line poem in iambic tetrameter, has a rhyme scheme of *abab, cdcd, efef.* Appearing in print for the first time in Peck's first poetry anthology (*Sounds and Silences*, 1970), the poem reflects Peck's longing for travel as well as his attachment to the plains of his native Illinois and his love for his father. The poem begins:

> My father was the first to hear
> The passage of the geese each fall,
> Passing above the house so near
> He'd hear within his heart their call.

And ends with:

> Seeing them pass before the moon,
> Recalling the lure of faroff things.[5]

Not a great piece of poetry: some lines, such as the fourth one, a bit forced perhaps; the passing before the moon image a bit clichéd. But the poem portrays a sensitive male image—something Peck believes to be very important—and leaves the reader with a pensive, perhaps melancholy, feeling.

The saddest poem he has ever published—perhaps the saddest thing he has ever written about—is a reaction to the effects of the shootings and bombings in Northern Ireland. Entitled "Irish Child," it describes a place "Where children learn to walk again on stumps" and one child envisions a heaven of "froth-cloud seas, / . . . Where whole-limbed children run, / . . . to the very ramparts / Of heaven" where they gaze through unshattered windows "Out upon blue and more blue." Its message is as appropriate today as it was when it was first published in the *Chicago Tribune Magazine* in 1972.[6]

Sounds and Silences: Poetry for Now was the second major work that Richard Peck published. As a teacher at Hunter, Peck—like so many good English teachers—was in the habit of supplementing the traditional classroom fare by duplicating copies of contemporary poems in an effort to involve his disinterested students. "We weren't using textbooks at that point; we were using paperbacks," Peck recalls. "But all of the paperback collections were filled with old poetry in the public domain that could be obtained free [by publishers]. I wanted to introduce my students to poets living in their own time and using their own language." Half seriously, he reveals that he compiled this collection "because I was illegally mimeographing contemporary poetry and handing it out to my kids." "Besides," he adds, "I was tired of having purple fingers."

Sounds and Silences, consisting of 104 poems, is divided into twelve sections on topics that dominated the concerns of the youth of those Vietnam years: Illusion, Dissent, War, Love, Communications, as well as topics that have concerned all people throughout time, such as Identity, Isolation, Childhood, and the Family. "Here's a glimpse of the feel, a touch of the smell, an echo of the thought of this age," wrote a reviewer in the *Christian Science Monitor*.[7] "The tempo is definitely now," stated the *Saturday Review*.[8]

Included are song lyrics by John Lennon and Paul McCartney, Malvina Reynolds, Leonard Cohen, and Pete Seeger, along with some traditional poems included in school anthologies by poets such as Robert Frost, Langston Hughes, and Theodore Roethke. There are also names that were likely new to both students and teachers then, among them Donald Hall, Brooks Jenkins, Philip Larkin, and Russell Atkins, mixed in with poets whose works are now almost as frequently anthologized as the works of earlier masters: Gwendolyn Brooks, Randall Jarrell, James Dickey, May Swenson, LeRoi Jones, and Denise Levertov. And, naturally, there was one poem by Peck himself, "The Geese," described earlier in this chapter.

Although reviewers in *Kirkus* and *The Grade Teacher* noted that this anthology did not have the visual appeal of a collection such as *Reflections on a Gift of Watermelon Pickle*, the most popular poetry anthology of the 1970s, *Kirkus* found it to be comparable in quality. And John W. Conner, writing in the September 1971 *English Journal*, declared it to be "the most exciting collection of verse" he had read that year.[9] One of the most important characteristics that Conner noted was the brevity of the poems that makes them easier for readers to study and enables teachers to introduce several poems on the same theme in one class period. Also significant to the anthology's success was its immediate availability in paperback, a form Peck preferred so that teachers could afford to buy classroom sets—which they did.

Encouraged by the extensive and enthusiastic reviews of *Sounds and Silences*, Dell approved a second anthology, which was published the following year. Much like its predecessor, *Mindscapes: Poems for the Real World* consists of eighty-six poems, most of them first published in the 1960s, grouped into eleven categories titled with lines taken from poems in those sections. Among them are "The Brick Bench outside the House," "A Paw on the Sill," "A Design of White Bones," and "These Naked Iron Muscles Dripping Oil." These poems, Peck writes in the introduction, stress "the real over the ideal, the compassionate over the sentimental," while enabling readers to explore "the landscapes of the mind . . . moving both writer and reader out into wider fields, all ripe for further discovery."

Although there are a few familiar poems in this book—for example, Housman's "To an Athlete Dying Young," Frost's "Out, Out—," and Robinson's "Mr. Flood's Party"—there are also poems that were unfamiliar to most people at the time: poems about astronauts and cowboys, bums and lovers, sharks and movie monsters, with new interpretations—sometimes jarring ones—of the "old time-honored themes of love, death, and nature." As Peck intended, these are poems through which readers can encounter "a real, hectic, unpretty, and recognizable world."

Among such well-known older poets as Walt Whitman and A. E. Housman, and popular modern poets such as John Ciardi and William Carlos Williams, are the sixties' poets Lawrence Ferlinghetti and Rod McKuen, newer poets of note today, including May Swenson, William Stafford, John Updike, Galway Kinnell, and Mari Evans, and a few lesser-known poets. In addition, Peck includes two of his own, previously unpublished, poems: "Jump Shot" and "Mission Uncontrolled."

Although Walter Clemons, reviewing *Mindscapes* for the *New York*

Times Book Review, concluded that this collection contains "too many easy, sentimental messages" presented "in open forms and plain language that dogs and cats can read,"[10] other reviewers found it to be "absorbing," "fresh and uncompromising" (*Kirkus Reviews*),[11] an "inviting, quality poetry anthology" (*Booklist*),[12] and "a good addition to high school poetry shelves" (*Library Journal*).[13]

Pictures That Storm Inside My Head, published in 1976 only in paperback (by Avon), follows the successful pattern Peck established in his previous anthologies—except that the poems in this collection are a bit more sophisticated than those in the earlier collections. Was that intentional? Peck says, "No, I think it just worked out that way. It was probably that old school teacher in me who was saying: 'Now that you've been at one level, let's move on to the next.'"

Reviews were scarcer on this collection, due probably to its not being first published in hardcover, and it took longer to become known. *Booklist* gave it a starred review and expected it to have "wide appeal for teenage poetry lovers";[14] *School Library Journal* did not review it until half a year later but also predicted it would be as popular as the first two collections;[15] and the Salt Lake City *Deseret News*, reviewing it only after Richard Peck had spoken at a meeting of the Utah Library Association in 1981, called the book "contemporary and fresh."[16]

As the book's title indicates, all of the poems illustrate storms of some kind: some are vicious, some are unexpected, and some, no matter what their form, help clear the air. This is a collection, the anthologist points out, that is about thinking young, remembering how exciting and how painful it was, "how grim it was to be imprisoned in childhood, how wonderful it was to know you were in love, how awful it was not to be able to say it, how good and terrible first things were."[17] But only a few selections are from a young person's perspective—for example, "Corner" by Ralph Pomeroy and "Cherrylog Road" by James Dickey, along with "Birdsong," reprinted from *I Never Saw Another Butterfly,* the wrenchingly beautiful poem by an unnamed child in the Terezin concentration camp who exclaimed in 1941: "how wonderful it is / To be alive."[18]

Divided into nine sections and a single endpiece, under such headings as "a ten-clawed monster," "touch me if you can," "it is sometimes summer," and "why don't you write," this anthology mirrors its predecessors in its types of poems and its scope. There is a mixture of the famous—Robert Penn Warren, Nikki Giovanni, e. e. cummings, and Anne Sexton—and the not so famous—Lou Lipsitz, Adrien Stoutenburg, Sandra Hochman, Kalungano, Anthony Ostroff, and Peck's own "Nancy." A few titles are familiar to most teachers— "Birches" by Robert Frost and "Sniper" by Robert Francis—but most were not widely known at the time of publication and are not especially familiar to the average person even today.

A Tucson librarian, Sarajean Marks, concluded her *School Library Journal* review of *Pictures That Storm* with the same kind of comment made so often about Richard Peck's novels: "Peck has an uncanny knack for knowing the tastes of teenagers."[19] Unfortunately, educators and librarians have to rely on what copies they already possess in their bookrooms or on their library shelves, since all three of these volumes are out of print. However, Dell intends to reissue *Sounds and Silences* possibly in 1990.

Richard Peck subtly educates readers to the pleasures and uses of poetry by including an entire poem or at least some verse in almost every one of his young adult novels. Three types of poetic forms are evident in those works: lines by famous poets, doggerel, and serious poems—Peck writing both of the latter two types. "I don't just stop the novel and say, 'I'd like you to read some of my poetry,'" Peck declares. "It just always happens to fit in, one way or another."

Peck began that practice with his very first novel for young adults. Early in *Don't Look and It Won't Hurt*, Carol, the narrator, recalls a childhood poem she and her younger sister had memorized years earlier, when life was simpler: "Little Donkey Close Your Eyes" by Margaret Wise. Later, when her pregnant older sister Ellen leaves for Chicago, "going off alone to have a baby she'd have to give away to strangers," Carol recalls some lines from the Beatles's song "She's Leaving Home."

Lines about death from Tennyson's "Crossing the Bar" and John Donne's "Death Be Not Proud" are quoted in *Dreamland Lake*, along with two entire poems: Maurice Sagoff's "Frankenstein by Mary W. Shelley" (a poem that Peck reprinted three years later in *Pictures*

That Storm Inside My Head) and Reed Whittemore's "The High School Band" (which Peck had included in *Mindscapes* two years before). Also on the topic of death, at the funeral of Byron and Jim Atwater's mother in *Father Figure*, the minister quotes four lines from Milton's *Samson Agonistes*: "Nothing is here for tears . . ."

Conrad Aiken's poem "Music I Heard with You" that ends with "All that was once so beautiful is dead" appears in *Representing Super Doll*. In *Are You in the House Alone?* Gail is unnerved by the Wordsworth poem her English class is studying: "Strange Fits of Passion I Have Known." Gerard Manley Hopkins's poem that begins "Margaret are you grieving / Over Goldengrove unleaving?" and ends with "Sorrow's springs are the same" plays a symbolic role in *Close Enough to Touch*. And a cub newspaper reporter in *The Ghost Belonged to Me* quotes two Longfellow lines to Alexander Armsworth: "A town that boasts inhabitants like me / Can have no lack of good society."

William Shakespeare has served Richard Peck's purposes in several instances. Peck uses two lines from *Antony and Cleopatra* in *Through a Brief Darkness* to portend forthcoming unpleasantness: "The bright day is done, / And we are for the dark." In *Are You in the House Alone?* Gail's boyfriend Steve gives her a copy of several lines from *Othello*, beginning with "My heart is turn'd to stone." Peck uses Shakespeare most extensively in *The Dreadful Future of Blossom Culp*. In that novel, Blossom is frequently quoting lines from *Hamlet* to illustrate a point or explore an issue, including the expected "To be or not to be" as well as "There is nothing either good or bad, but thinking makes it so." Of course, by the end of the novel, every time Alexander hears Blossom spout anything poetic, he knows it must be from *Hamlet*.

Given Peck's quick wit, it is not surprising to find several instances of verse being used to make readers smile. And in this second category, the proper term for much of that verse is *doggerel*, since the term *poetry* gives it too much status. On the cover of a student's notebook in *The Dreadful Future of Blossom Culp*, for example, are these immortal words: "If you love me as I love you, / No knife can cut our love in two." Blossom's teacher, Miss Fuller, obviously love-struck, reads a pair of couplets that aren't much better than the notebook scribbling. Blossom is convinced that Miss Fuller "had no doubt cribbed it off a two-cent valentine." (Remember, that was 1914.) Peck really did lift that from a two-cent Valentine card from that era. Similar doggerel also appears in other novels. In *Princess Ashley* as well as in *Remembering the Good Times* there are school cheers from the pep squad and cheerleaders—Peck's paraphrases of real cheers. In *Father Figure*, Jim and Byron rent bicycles from a store with the following sign in the window:

> Buy a car nevermore
> Remember: Ten on the sprocket
> Not four on the floor

a sign that Peck had observed in a real store window in Coconut Grove, Florida, when he was writing *Father Figure*. In *Representing Super Doll*, the school newspaper prints a hurtful couplet about Darlene. Even more hurtful is the verse scrawled on the mirror of the sixth-grade girls' washroom in *Through a Brief Darkness*:

> Andreas daddys a fireman
> Carmens fathers a cook
> Rachaels dad is a doctor
> But Karens old man is a CROOK

Other appearances of verse occur in *Ghosts I Have Been* (two stanzas about the Titanic disaster in which Peck delightfully rhymes "floating flotsam" with "wondrous Blossom") and in *Blossom Culp and the Sleep of Death* (a chant by an Egyptian princess).

Some of the most enjoyable lines are those made (courtesy of Richard Peck) by Pod, the lovable oddball in *Princess Ashley*. The novel contains several of Pod's poetic efforts, such as the following: "*Gimme my red-eye gravy, my Coors, and my grits / And a day in the saddle till it hurts where I sits.*" Chelsea sympathetically calls this Pod's "Nashville period."

There are others, too—not intended to be funny. Gail receives a poem from her boyfriend Steve in *Are You in the House Alone?* that begins "I'll be so gentle you won't know I'm there." In *Remembering the Good Times*, during tryouts for a part in *The Glass Menagerie*,

Kate reads a poem that Travis had written. It begins: "The days of winter enter in, / The Darkness nibbles at the days," and goes on to foreshadow Travis's suicide.

Perhaps the poems that most challenged Richard Peck occur in *Princess Ashley.* Not only did Peck have to come up with several instances of doggerel that could be realistically attributable to Pod, but he also had to construct poems that an "angry, introverted fifteen-year-old girl" was supposed to have written. The most revealing of those poems is entitled "Girl in the Mirror," two of the key lines from which are: "I'd like to read her mind and look her in the eye, / I'd like to know her better but I'm shy." Reading those lines early in the novel, the reader, just like Chelsea, is convinced they belong to Ashley.

Peck's most ambitious effort to use poetry in a fictional work can be found in an as-yet-unpublished short story he wrote during the summer of 1988. In "I Go Along," nonacademically oriented Gene explains how he got himself invited along with a gifted junior class to attend a poetry reading at a local college. On the school bus ride there he meets Sharon, a likable girl who seems to understand what he does not. Seeing a living poet for the first time, Gene is surprised: "he's not dressed like a poet. In fact, he's dressed like me: Levi's and Levi jacket. Big heavy-duty belt buckle. Boots, even. . . . It's weird, like there could be poets around and you wouldn't realize they were there." For the poetry that the speaker reads, Peck wrote two poems, one about a man watching his wife sleep, and another called "High School," in which a student dreams his worst fears, including forgetting his locker combination, being cut from the team, and someone tampering with the bell on the last period on Friday so the bell won't ring. Gene concludes that the others were poems but that last one wasn't: "'You can't write poems about zits and your locker combination.'" Sharon responds: "'Maybe nobody told the poet that.'"

At least nobody told Richard Peck that. Of course, Richard Peck insists, "I am not a poet."

6. Early Novels

When Richard Peck faced the mute green keys of his Royal typewriter at the start of the summer of 1971, he had only a vague idea of his direction. He was determined to write a novel. He knew he wanted to write for teenagers, because that was the audience he knew from his years of teaching. He surely had things he wanted to say to kids, though he knew he could not preach to them. And he felt strongly that he did not want to write about his own personal experiences. Moreover, "I knew I couldn't tell it about the kids that I had just come from in teaching," he says, "because I was overheated on that subject. I was not only burned out but I was also a bit angry. I was too close to it."

In looking for a story outside of his own experiences, Peck began to think about the young pregnant girls he had met at the home of friends in Evanston, Illinois. There a doctor and his wife—Richard and Jean Hughes—took into their home girls from a local home for unmarried mothers-to-be, making them part of the family and providing a pleasant environment for them. "Each time I visited them, I would meet another girl waiting to have a baby," Peck recalls. "In those days, homes for unwed mothers were more heavily populated than they are today." Asking his friends if they observed a pattern, anything the girls had in common, he learned there was a clear profile: "They all say they will keep the baby; they all say they will marry the father; they all say they will never go home to their community. We follow up and find they all give up the baby; none of them marry the father or have the opportunity to; and they all go back home." With that information, Peck was ready to write.

"Books at their most worthwhile are the success stories of people who manage to prevail in trying times.... And the survivors are those who have taken independent action."[1] That statement was written by Peck for the dust jacket of *Princess Ashley,* but it could have been said also about his first novel as well as every one Peck has written since.

Although *Don't Look and It Won't Hurt* began as a story about an unmarried pregnant teenager, Peck developed it into something more significant than a tract about characteristics and problems of teenage pregnancy. It's a novel about responsibility, the disintegration of a rural, small-town family, and human relationships: mother–daughter, sister–sister, father–daughter, boy–girl.

Carol Patterson, not quite sixteen years old, is the middle sister in a poor family without a father. So she watches as her irresponsible seventeen-year-old sister Ellen falls for a twenty-year-old guy who says he's helping draft evaders escape to Canada during the Vietnam War, when in fact he's a drug dealer who is soon arrested and sent to prison for ten years. And because their mother works the evening shift at the restaurant near the interstate on the edge of their small Illinois town, Carol feels responsible for her nine-year-old sister, Liz. Their father is a ne'er-do-well who left the family years ago (but who does help Carol at one point later in the story). Their mother seems overwhelmed by her inability to control her daughters' lives in the face of her own unsuccessful life. Carol feels she must be the one to hold the family together. She even turns down a romance with a local boy because she feels there isn't "much future in it." She wants a better life than what affable and complacent Jerry can provide in a town like Claypitts. After Ellen leaves for Chicago to have the baby, she communicates only with Carol, and that rarely. Fearing her sister won't ever come back home, Carol eventually takes the overnight bus to try to find her sister and talk her into returning.

This is a rather dark novel for a writer who has become known for his humor. It's not about suburban youngsters as many of Peck's books are; there are no gimmicks, such as ghosts or shopping malls—"they don't even go to a party in this one," Peck notes, although there is an exciting car wreck; no one rescues the girls and makes their life better in the end; in fact, there are no clear resolutions in the novel, a fact that disappointed the reviewer for *Library Journal*.[2] It isn't certain, for example, that Ellen will return home after the baby is born, though she probably will; there is no indication that Carol will pursue the contact she has made with her father or that it will be advantageous to do so; the stray cat that Liz has brought home is at the vet, with no promise that its injured leg will heal; and Carol is still the sister in the middle feeling responsible. The only character besides Carol who seems to have changed and become a little more understanding in the final scene is the mother, though her relative tenderness and nonjudgmental response when Carol returns from Chicago is a bit too pat to be completely realistic. Nevertheless, the reviewer for *Booklist* found the novel "real and affecting."[3] What this sensitive novel does show is that Carol has come to understand herself and others better, and that, after all, is a realistic and satisfying outcome. As in real life, there are a lot of raw edges in this novel.

Although *Kirkus*'s review wasn't very complimentary,[4] *Publishers Weekly* proclaimed this "an extraordinarily good" first novel,[5] and most other reviews gave it supportive comments. A surprising negative response came several years later in a book about teaching adolescent literature. Educator Sheila Schwartz, who herself has written novels for teenagers as well as adults, proclaimed Peck's first novel "poor adolescent literature" because it "contains no concepts of value for the teenager today."[6] Believing that the novel's key message tells readers to close their eyes to painful things, Schwartz concludes that Peck is giving young people "a potentially harmful philosophical perception."[7] No other reviewers interpreted the title that way, nor do letters that Richard Peck receives from students. In contrast to the book's title, the theme of individual responsibility is unmistakably evident.

That same theme of individual responsibility lies beneath the mysterious elements of Richard Peck's second novel, *Dreamland Lake*. The book is also about death and friendship and life in a small

Midwestern town. Whether or not the story can be classified as a mystery is debatable. The Edgar Allan Poe Mystery Award selection committee obviously thought it a mystery in 1973. Many of the letters that Peck receives about this book certainly interpret it as a mystery. The novel opens with two boys discovering a decomposed body at the edge of a lake where an amusement park had once been. And there are several mysterious events related to a classmate's behavior throughout the novel. But Peck did not intend the story to be a mystery, he maintains. In fact, the narrator of the story says on the second page: "If some of [the story] sounds like a murder mystery or something, remember, it isn't." Rather than quibble, it's wiser to adopt the approach of the *School Library Journal* reviewer who wrote that readers will be "captivated first by the mystery, and then by its deeper levels of meaning."[8]

It does not matter how the old man died, only that his remains are discovered by two seventh graders, Brian and Flip (Philip), and that they are observed by a friendless classmate, Elvan Helligrew. Fat Elvan, like "a damn big dog that hangs around waiting for you to kick it," goes to unusual lengths to get attention. Evan's main passion is for Nazi memorabilia: helmet, flag, sword, insignia, almost anything with a swastika on it. Flip is a leader, often doing senseless things; Brian follows, unprotesting. Both, looking for adventure, find more than they bargained for.

Beginning with the dead tramp, the story recounts Brian's loss of innocence as it progresses through other deaths—old Mrs. Garrison's son, a van accident on the highway, the boy who fell from the railroad bridge—ending with the horrifying death of Elvan. Brian, recounting the story and acknowledging his guilt, blames Flip for what happened but blames himself for following. From the perspective of two years after the event, Brian says, "I might have been able to change things for all of us, for Elvan too. But I didn't see it then. I wasn't really ready to stop being a follower." The death of Elvan marks the end of the friendship between Brian and Flip; in fact, in an additional sad note, Brian says that he hasn't had a close friend since.

In spite of its grim ending and somber theme, there is some humor throughout the rest of the novel, with lively glimpses at the boys' paper route adventures and a description of their English class. The

adventures come in rapid succession with enough evident foreshadowing to keep normally reluctant readers moving through the story.
Reviewers praised the "finely tuned"[9] novel's "emotional depth,"[10]
and "superior . . . characterizations."[11] In addition, the relationship
between the boys, with its "ambiguous mixture of nostalgia and
guilt," reminded reviewers for *Kirkus*[12] and *Booklist*[13] of John
Knowles's *A Separate Peace*. Not only were all the major reviews supportive, but letters Peck receives have consistently reflected the involvement of readers, most of them boys. Because of those letters,
Peck feels that *Dreamland Lake* is one of his best books, in spite
of—or perhaps because of—the fact that many of the letter writers
resist the message of the book. Peck explains:

> They say, "I don't understand the book," but you can tell from the
> letters that they do. They don't *accept* the message. I believe in
> books that incite to riot, and *Dreamland Lake* is just disturbing
> enough to get a rise out of the reader. Of course it's because I was a
> teacher: you're always trying to get them to feel passionately about
> something.

Thinking independently is not a major theme in Peck's third novel
for young adults, but it is a significant element in it. Sixteen-year-old
Karen Beatty, motherless daughter of a big-time New York mobster,
has always done what her father or his secretary have told her. Forced
to attend boarding schools—she's "a veteran of a whole catalogue of
schools and camps"—she remains blind to her father's shady activities. Her complaisance allows her to be easily kidnapped and flown to
London, supposedly to stay with cousins whom she has never seen
before. Karen does not know that her father has been attacked by
rival mobsters who set him afire; he remains in a coma in the hospital. Learning that her "cousins" are agents of her father's enemies,
she vows to get to the bottom of the mystery. "There'd already been
too many times in her life when she'd been expected to follow
blindly." Enlisting the aid of a childhood friend who happens to be
studying at Eton and assisted by an old woman who appears fortuit-
ously, she makes her escape. Ultimately, though, she must act independently in order to survive. Karen's friend, Jay, is also seeking

independence from his domineering parents. Before the novel's end, he vows to rebel against his parents' expectations of what he should do with his life. And in the end, the far-wiser Karen is united with her father in New York City, with a clearer understanding of how she will act in the future and an acceptance of who she is.

Suspense is a key factor in this novel. Peck establishes it early and maintains it effectively to the very end, thus keeping the novel moving rapidly. The hint of romance adds to the adventure. And glimpses of London and the British countryside, as well as a description of a rough crossing of the English channel, provide a depth to the setting that few other young adult novels offer. However, as one reviewer noted, the extensive description of Jay's life at Eton seems out of place and unnecessary.[14]

The plotting in this novel is more contrived than that in any of Peck's other books, except perhaps for *Amanda/Miranda*. But Peck intended both novels to be basically Gothic adventure-romances, which traditionally employ melodrama and rely to some extent on stereotyped characters as well as chance encounters between characters and events. In *Through a Brief Darkness*, Jay just happens to be studying at Eton and happens to be in London at the right time; his parents just happen to be visiting at exactly that moment; when Jay helps Karen escape from her captors initially, they retreat to the family home of Desmond Hoaresham-D'ark, Jay's "boy" (a first-year student at Eton), but instead of finding the house empty, Jay's grandmother happens to be there; and in spite of having had no previous contact with these two American teenagers, Mrs. Hoaresham calmly and completely takes over the management of Karen's escape. A critical reader, therefore, has the choice of faulting Peck for his contrived plotting and stereotyped characters, as the *School Library Journal* reviewer did,[15] or praising him for writing "a tightly drawn romantic melodrama" that "wisely relinquishes any pretense to relevance or depth," as the *Kirkus* reviewer did.[16]

Peck himself says that after writing two serious teenage novels, he wanted to write something light, a "page-turner," combining the elements of a young adult novel with those of a Gothic romance. "I believe in books for increasing pleasure of reading books," he says. Assuming he had accomplished what he had set out to do, Peck expected no letters about *Through a Brief Darkness*. But young readers had a deeper reaction to the novel than Peck expected they would. The letter writers, Peck says, "are very caught up in the relationship . . . between the girl and her father. . . . I thought that the fact that the father and the daughter could not communicate in here simply set up the plot. . . . But they don't see it that way." "That taught me something," Peck admits: "that my opinion doesn't really count here. And that's okay. They're helping to write the novel, a novel that's far from my intent." Nevertheless, much of Peck's intent remains evident to most readers.

What is not evident is the story behind this novel, though Richard Peck has told it to various audiences. His landlord—unintentionally, of course—provided the model for the gangland incident in this novel. When he started writing novels, Peck was renting the carriage house behind his landlord's big house in Brooklyn. One day on his way to work, the man was set on fire. His wife then revealed that her husband was in the Mafia. Later, after the man was beaten on the steps of his house, the family sold the property and left abruptly. In addition to worrying about where he was going to live, Peck began to think about his former landlord's teenage daughter. "What would it be like to have everything one day and then be on the run the next?" he wondered. The adults could fend for themselves, he concluded; but what about that teenage daughter? And that question provided the impetus for *Through a Brief Darkness*.

Although there is adventure in *Representing Super Doll*, the action is not life-threatening. This ALA Best Book for Young Adults explores the topic of female beauty—contrasting one sixteen-year-old who has it with one who does not. Reviewers praised the "natural, often snappy dialogue and convincing characterizations"[17] of this "swift, funny, and touching story."[18] Zena Sutherland emphasized the book's "vitality and flow," along with "a fresh viewpoint . . . and a deeper treatment of a theme than most beauty contest books achieve."[19] But Jean Alexander in the *Washington Post*, believing that the beautiful Darlene and not the "smug" Verna is the heroine of the novel, states that Peck "fails to make his point."[20]

It is difficult to decide who the main character is in *Representing Super Doll*, and Peck acknowledges that himself. The novel is about

Darlene Hoffmeister, "the dumbest, most beautiful girl that anyone ever heard of," but it's narrated by Verna Henderson, a level-headed, intelligent, "country mouse." Peck asks rhetorically: "Is Verna the heroine of the novel or is she the protagonist? Is she watching other people live or is she telling you the whole story of her life?" It is fruitless to argue about who the main character is because both girls are needed to explore the theme of this novel: "the terrible tyranny of glamour."[21] Peck says about Verna:

> She didn't *mean* to be having an adventure of her own; she meant to tell you about this girl she went to school with . . . but of course she has to get involved, otherwise she's too much the author standing in the wings. And then she learns a few things about herself. But she's still the kind of person who is more interested in other people than in herself. And that turns out to be a wonderfully subtle narrator.

It is clear to Verna that although Darlene looks gorgeous she is miserable because of what she has to go through, both with her classmates and in public appearances, when she wins the title of Miss Hybrid Seed Corn and then the Central United States Teen Super Doll beauty contest. Verna, though never jealous of Darlene's beauty, is not the unglamorous country girl seeking acceptance in the high school of Peck's fictional Midwestern town of Dunthorpe.

A three-day public relations trip to New York, on which Verna accompanies Darlene, is the turning point in both girls' lives. As part of the tour, Darlene is scheduled to appear on the television panel show "Spot the Frauds" (patterned after the real "To Tell the Truth" on which Richard Peck used to appear as an impostor). Verna, at the last minute, must substitute for a missing Teen Super Doll imposter. Because she is viewed, as one panelist says, as "the kind of girl who would be chosen to represent young people," Verna fools everyone, while Darlene appears to have nothing but good looks going for her. Verna comes to realize that her intelligence is worth far more than Darlene's beauty and that, with a new hairdo and the right clothes, she is more attractive than she ever imagined.

In the process of visiting New York City, Verna sees a world that is much wider than her small Midwestern community, and she is anxious to explore it in the future. And in the end, Darlene possesses enough sense to realize that she has been unhappily doing what her pushy mother wants for her and refuses to enter any further beauty contests. Thus, finding one's identity and making independent decisions are once again significant themes in this novel.

Although Darlene comes from a "broken home," Verna lives within an old-fashioned, hard-working farm family with a strong but sensitive father, a sensitive but strong mother, a supportive older brother, and an aunt who is somewhat cantankerous but lovable as well. (In fact, Aunt Eunice is the most colorful adult character in the novel.) Here Peck may well be making a comment about the preference of farm life over city life. Certainly a traditional family with a mother, a father, and two children (one of each sex) reflects an earlier concept of the ideal American family.

This is also a lighter book with more humorous scenes than Peck produced in any of his first three novels (though none of them is without humorous incidents). Particularly funny are the scenes when Verna's four friends from town visit her farm home and when Verna and Darlene go to New York City and have to deal with taxis, subways, bag ladies, nasty waitresses, restaurants that "don't do malteds," and television news programs that specialize in violent crimes (and prompts Verna to say, "I just sat there feeling privileged to be left alive"). Richard Peck's next novel was to be even lighter and more humorous, its success leading to a string of novels about the now infamous Blossom Culp.

7. The Blossom Culp Novels

Almost all ghost stories have interesting origins, and Peck's first ghost story is no exception. There was nothing supernatural about how he came to write *The Ghost Belonged to Me*, but the evolution of the novel and what followed it involve the intersection of a number of forces.

By the time he had completed his fourth book for young adults, Richard Peck was eager to write about something other than today's youth culture. By that time also, he had been receiving letters from teenage readers and talking with groups of students across the country for some time. One of the letters, from a boy, asked Peck why he had never written a ghost story. Kids love ghost stories. And in talking with junior high school students, Peck found out that lots of boys knew all about the *Titanic* disaster. In addition, he thought he would write about the relationship between a young boy and an old man—"a young boy just entering life and an old man he admires who is just leaving life."[1]

As he gets ready to write a new novel, Peck says, he reviews the characteristics of his previous novels and tries to list ways in which he wants the new novel to be different. So his list at this point included a ghost, the *Titanic*, an old man and a young boy, and the past versus the present. As he told interviewer Paul Janeczko: "Originally the novel was to be a love story between a contemporary New York baseball-playing boy and the ghost of a girl who was killed on the *Titanic.* . . . When they finally confronted each other, the story fell apart."[2]

So Peck started over, dropping the love story, retaining the old man-young boy relationship, saving the *Titanic* incident for another time, and setting it entirely in the early 1900s in Bluff City, Peck's imaginary re-creation of his hometown of Decatur, Illinois, at the turn of the century. He also made it a comedy. "I'd rather write comedy than not," he says.

Somewhere during the development of his story about Alexander Armsworth and his Great-Uncle Miles, Peck realized something more was needed. He looked up from his typewriter, he says, "and there in the door stood Blossom Culp."[3] Later Blossom remarked that because "a boy gets into more scrapes than he can get out of," Alexander "just naturally need[ed] me to steer him right."[4] After *The Ghost Belonged to Me* was published in 1975, Richard Peck was surprised to receive more letters about Blossom than about Alexander Armsworth, the main character in the novel. Thus in the next novel, published two years later, Blossom became the main character, while Alexander became a side-kick and the sinking of the *Titanic* resurfaced as a key incident. And *Ghosts I Have Been* outsold its predecessor. Two other Blossom Culp novels followed during the next seven years, interspersed between Peck's more serious contemporary novels.

Blossom is "the poorest, plainest, most bedraggled girl" in Bluff City.[5] She's also the ugliest. She has big, nearly black, round eyes, dark kinky hair, and legs so skinny that Alexander says she has "a spidery look." Her drunken father left town long ago; her witchy, toothless mother is a fortune-teller for the most part—she "sees the Unseen." Blossom and her mother live in a decrepit two-room row house on the other side of the tracks. Above all, Blossom ranks among the spunkiest characters in contemporary literature for children and young adults. "I've always lived by my wits," she says.

In spite of having illiterate parents, Blossom is, as she puts it, "a quick study." While her grammar isn't perfect and clichés abound in her tales, she's an excellent speller, even though she spends as little time in school as possible. Her language is colorful and clever, her voice a combination of the countrified female voices Richard Peck heard from his relatives in Illinois.[6] Most important, she has not only inherited her mother's clairvoyant ability, but Blossom's talents are even greater—for in the four novels in which she appears, she travels both backward and forward in time.

The supernatural is one of the most popular topics with teenagers today. But rather than leaning toward the horror in the supernatural, Peck finds comedy in it. "[I]t is a relief to occasionally turn to" Peck's Blossom Culp novels because of their comic elements, say Nilsen and Donelson in their text on young adult literature.[7] Moreover, they note, Blossom uses her supernatural talents not to hurt others (well, maybe Letty Shambaugh a little) but "to become more and more compassionate."[8] Blossom's purpose in traveling through time is always to help or comfort someone in distress.

Barbara Elleman, editor of children's book reviews for both *Learning* magazine and *Booklist*, in 1985 proclaimed *The Ghost Belonged to Me* one of the "50 Books Too Good to Be Missed" from the past twenty years.[9] *Booklist* called it a "wholly entertaining . . . hair raising" comedy,[10] while *School Library Journal* declared it "a light romp with engaging characters, plenty of laughs, and enough shivery moments to qualify as a mystery too."[11] *The Junior Bookshelf* called Blossom "a splendid creation."[12] Reviews in the *New York Times* and *Psychology Today* were more critical, declaring the voice of thirteen-year-old Alexander "unsteady, rarely evoking the feelings of a child,"[13] and Alexander's parents "flat, predictable," cartoon characters.[14]

Granted, none of the parents in any of the Blossom Culp novels provides a positive model, though from a feminist point of view one librarian proclaimed Blossom's mother to be "the most truly liberated woman in Peck's books" because she "does not one jot of housework, reads her future in tea leaves, throws the dregs on the floor, puts her feet upon the table, and goes to sleep."[15]

Although the most interesting adults in Richard Peck's novels are often old women, the most interesting adult in this novel is an old man: Alexander's great-uncle. Uncle Miles, patterned closely after Peck's real great-uncle by the same name, is a free-spirited, eighty-five-year-old carpenter "who's lived just the way he's wanted to" and who knows everything about everybody else's business. It is Uncle Miles who knows the history of the Armsworth mansion, because he built it for a former riverboat captain in 1861. Thus it is Uncle Miles's story about Captain Thibodaux that explains the ghost of young Inez Dumaine and her damp dog that haunt the brick barn. And it is Uncle Miles who accompanies Alexander to New Orleans (with Blossom tagging along) in order to give Inez a proper burial with the rest of her relatives.

In the process, the ghost of Inez informs Alexander about a tragedy about to happen with a train, and a bridge, and a man with one hand. As a result, Alexander becomes famous because he saves the lives of passengers on the trolley. There is another subplot that involves Alexander's sister Lucille, her boyfriend Tom Hackett, and an enterprising newspaper reporter who becomes attracted to Lucille. Lucille's coming out party provides the opportunity for some slapstick humor, though Blossom's comments and actions provide smiles and chuckles whenever she appears.

In visiting schools around the country, Richard Peck sometimes finds himself with an unresponsive group of students. Desperate to find a topic of interest to a group of eighth graders one time, he mentioned the *Titanic*. "Boy, that room really came alive," he recalls. "They knew everything about it! It was their favorite disaster. So I began to read up on it, just to have a fallback topic when all else failed."[16] He used that information in his first adult novel, *Amanda/Miranda*, and made it a focal point in *Ghosts I Have Been*.

Having discovered Blossom's popularity, Peck wisely wrote the second book in her voice. Later, Blossom remarked that although he had made "a grave error by letting Alexander tell the [first] story, . . . Mr. Peck had the sense to step aside and let me tell this story . . . in my own way."[17]

In the fall of 1913, a few months after the ending of *The Ghost Belonged to Me,* Blossom Culp describes herself as "a plain American girl with nothing going for me but spunk," who has "the talent for involving myself in other people's business." She gets involved in plenty. First she scares Alexander and his mischievous buddies on Halloween night as they attempt to overturn Old Man Leverette's outhouse. Then she is invited to an after-school meeting of The Sunny Thoughts

and Busy Fingers Sisterhood led by Letty Shambaugh where she first
fakes a "Second Sight" incident and then really does have a vision of a
boy being run over by an automobile—her first authentic experience
with Second Sight. She quickly has other visions of both past and future events, most of which she can't comprehend. One of them is a vision of World War I; in another she sees men walking on the moon.
"[A]lways an astute observer and critic of hidden motivations and
guarded sentiments," writes Tony Manna in The ALAN Review, Blossom uses these experiences to moralize about society—"each of her visions an increasingly intense indictment of a society gone and about to
go haywire."[18]

Invited to tea by the eccentric Miss Dabney, Blossom and
Alexander encounter the ghost of a serving girl who had hanged herself in the kitchen years earlier. Later, when Miss Dabney falls for
the scam of a charlatan who claims to hold seances with the dead,
Blossom finds a creative way to unmask the "professor."

Forced by her school principal, Miss Spaulding, to prove her ability to "see the Unseen," Blossom passes back nearly two years in time
to find herself aboard the sinking Titanic where she comforts a
young boy who is about to slip beneath the icy dark waters, and returns to reality with a wet blanket on which is woven the word Titanic. Both Blossom and the town become famous; Blossom's
mother's "business" flourishes; and Blossom receives a commenda-
tion from the Queen of England and an invitation to visit. With the
help and guidance of Miss Dabney, she meets Queen Mary and becomes "a footnote to history."

Everyone loved this novel; it earned best book of the year honors
from the American Library Association, School Library Journal, and
the New York Times; it eventually was named one of the ALA Young
Adult Services Division's "Best of the Best 1970–82"; and Walt Disney
Productions made a television movie out of it, entitled "Child of
Glass" (see Appendix B). School Library Journal praised the "hilari-
ous" first-person narration and its combination of "humor, occult adventure, and a thoroughly engaging heroine."[19] Horn Book singled out
the "unmistakable American accent" of this "effervescent comedy."[20]
And more than one reviewer likened Peck's style to that of Mark
Twain, although the Kliatt reviewer opined that "the wit and insight of

the narrator will be missed by most of the audience the book is intended for."[21] Maybe so—but that also suggests that adult readers might find this book as entertaining as young adults do.

Some reviewers found *The Dreadful Future of Blossom Culp* a letdown from its predecessor, mainly because its commentary on contemporary society is so negative. In contrast to the accolades received by *Ghosts I Have Been*, this one won no prizes.

In Peck's third Blossom Culp novel, Blossom is zapped through a timewarp from 1914 to 1984 to discover that Bluff City has become "one of your better upper-middle-class suburbs" called Bluffleigh and increased in population from 2,200 to 68,002. Except for meeting Jeremy, with whom she shares a mutual attraction, the rest of the world of the eighties is, as Blossom herself puts it, "a real interesting place to visit, but I wouldn't want to live there."[22] Jeremy, a solitary teenager from a broken home, spends most of his time playing computer games. His father lives in a singles condo complex; his mother is so busy with her own life that she doesn't even notice Blossom's presence. His sister Tiffany dresses punk, spends most of her life at the mall, and speaks Valley Girl argot—e.g. "like totally." Blossom finds her fascinating: "I never heard tell of a girl named for a lamp before," she says, "though this one was none too bright."

School in the eighties is a sham. The middle-school building is architecturally sterile. Attendance is optional. Kids who are reading "at or near grade level" are termed "Gifted," and everyone is "heavy into computer math." The classes are totally out of control because it's Halloween and everyone is in costume (which allows Blossom to attend in her own clothes)—though Blossom says, "I doubt things were much better on a regular day." Blossom's old high school has been replaced by a motel that advertises day rates and water beds. Blossom wisely wants to return to 1914.

That kind of commentary by Richard Peck led Patricia Lee Gauch, herself a young adult novelist, to conclude her review in the *New York Times Book Review* with: "Blossom is too good a character to end up chiefly a vehicle for social commentary on the sterility and loneliness of our contemporary adolescent world."[23]

In all fairness, though, there's much to smile at in those same scenes, where Blossom tries to comprehend the meaning of

Cuisinart and microwave, along with television in general and Pac-Man and Atari 2600 VCS in particular. Jeremy, in fact, is so far into video games that when Blossom first appears, he asks her: "What *game* are you from?"

Fortunately the eighties take up only about one-fourth of the book, with the rest being about Blossom and Alexander's other exploits in 1914 Bluff City. In the beginning of the novel, for example, Blossom once again foils the plans of Alexander and his cohorts, Bub and Champ, to victimize Old Man Leverette. In the process, Alexander is not only scared out of his wits but also gets a load of horse manure in his face. And in the end, while telling fortunes in the old haunted Leverette farmhouse, Blossom uses her talents to expose the duplicity of her history teacher, Mr. Ambrose Lacy. Teachers, in fact, receive a lot of attention in this novel, and Blossom quotes from *Hamlet* several times throughout the story.

Even though this book does not live up to the standards set by *Ghosts I Have Been*, it is still a fun read, providing "tons of gentle laughter that will charm even a punk rocker," said the *Ocala Star Banner*.[24] Ethel Heins in *Horn Book* praised the novel's "well-timed humorous repartee" and noted that "underlining everything is a perceptible human sensitivity."[25] And the *Parents' Choice* reviewer was delighted with the entire novel; she noted its "three belly laughs and two second-thoughts per chapter" and proclaimed it "one of the best teenage novels of the year."[26]

"After an uncomfortable brush with technology in *The Dreadful Future of Blossom Culp*, it is good to see our doughty heroine back where she belongs, in 1914," wrote Patty Campbell on the publication of Peck's fourth Blossom Culp book in 1986.[27] The American Library Association liked *Blossom Culp and the Sleep of Death* better than the previous one, too, naming it a Notable Book for Children. Other reviewers agreed. *School Library Journal*, for example, called it "an entertaining and generally well-crafted diversion with moments of inspired humor . . . and abundant examples of Peck's gift for turning the humorous phrase,"[28] and *Publishers Weekly* called it a "fast, feverish, funny, altogether satisfying escapade."[29]

Blossom tells readers that "Though the past and future are often open books to me, I have more trouble than most getting through the present." But in this novel, she deals adroitly with problems of both the present and the past. In the present, her rival Letty Shambaugh and her mother attempt to discredit the new ninth-grade history teacher, Miss Fairweather, because she was a suffragette and is therefore "a dangerous agitator." From the past appears the shade of Sat-Hathor, the daughter of the Egyptian goddess of love, who has been dead for nearly 4,000 years and whose tomb has been desecrated.

It just so happens that the ninth-grade history class is studying ancient Egypt. And although Blossom has recently accidentally burned down Old Man Leverette's privy with Alexander trapped inside it (he was ordered to stay in it, smoking a cigar, as part of a fraternity initiation), she convinces Alexander to work with her on a class project. Fighting all the way, Alexander tries to deny his talent of Second Sight, but soon, along with Blossom, gets involved with the *ka* or spirit of Sat-Hathor.

With clues discovered by both Alexander and Blossom's scavenging mother on the grounds of an abandoned circus on the edge of town, Blossom and Alexander locate the princess's mummy and some of her possessions. Then, after using them for their class project, they take them back in time and replace them safely in Sat-Hathor's tomb, scaring away grave-robbers in the process. Along the way, Blossom prevents Alexander from foolishly giving his fraternity pin to Letty Shambaugh; both Letty and her mother receive a surprising comeuppance that ties in perfectly with the rest of the story; Miss Fairweather attracts a male admirer; Blossom discovers that her talents for "seeing the Unseen" are greater than those of her disagreeable Mamma; and readers learn a lot about mummification and the desecration of Egyptian tombs. As Blossom might say, "The story's as busy as a swarm of flies on spilt chicken fat." Except she'd probably say it better.

Where will the indomitable Blossom turn up next? Peck isn't sure. "When she got to high school it opened up a whole new field of inquiry for her," Peck acknowledges. "Also, as she gets older, her feelings for Alexander are going to mature." How many books do you write in a series? Peck asks himself. "Do you want thirty of them, like Nancy Drew? I don't know how many more of those I can do. I think you need to know when to fold them, too."

8. Problem Novels

For most of the 1970s and into the early 1980s, the field of books for adolescents was dominated by "problem novels"—novels that explored contemporary topics that were easily categorized in bibliographies, such as drugs, divorce, physical handicaps, abortion, and death. The worst of those novels deal with a single topic in a manipulative or didactic manner, using shallow characters and arriving at an unrealistic solution. The best of them engage readers in a realistic, multidimensional story, with well-developed characters whose major problem is not necessarily resolved completely by the end of the story. In the decade between the mid-seventies and the mid-eighties, Richard Peck published four books that have often been classified as problem novels but that are clearly among the best of that type, mainly because they deal with multiple problems and they are so artfully written.

The differences between *Are You in the House Alone?, Father Figure, Close Enough to Touch,* and *Remembering the Good Times* and his first four novels are subtle ones. These later novels are more analytical and require the author to do a substantial amount of research—into the tell-tale signs of potential suicide, for example. Because they deal with topics that have a deeper emotional impact—such as being raped—they are more hard-hitting and contain little of Peck's usual humor. As a result these novels tend to appeal to a more mature audience. In addition, three of these four novels are set in the suburbs, where the majority of Peck's readers live.

Teenage rape is the focal problem in *Are You in the House Alone?*, though the book is also about friendships and communication, boy–girl relationships, parent–child relationships, student–educator relationships, and social class differences in a "snug, smug" Connecticut town. Gail, the sixteen-year-old victim and narrator, does not live in a vacuum, and the aftermath of her attack reveals the ways in which members of the community deal with it. The chief of police refuses to prosecute the attacker, Phil Lawver, because he is the son of the town's most prominent family; Gail's best friend, Alison, denies her own boyfriend's guilt; Gail's middle-class mother wants to put the whole incident behind her as quickly as possible; her father, recently laid-off from his job, feels powerless in his ability to protect his daughter or to bring the criminal to justice; the school guidance counselor is incapable of dealing with the problem or Gail's feelings about it because she's trained to deal only with test results; the mother for whom Gail babysits wants no more contact with Gail because she doesn't want to be reminded of what happened in her house; the lawyer is willing to take the case to court but he knows only too well that Gail is likely to be victimized again because she and her boyfriend have had a sexual relationship, because there were no witnesses, and because the accused rapist can plea-bargain to a lesser charge. The reader feels increasingly frustrated along with Gail who, Peck was certain to point out, did nothing to encourage the attack. It's not a pretty portrait, but it is truthful.

This is not to suggest that the novel is not entertaining. Peck avoids didacticism and creates a story that moves along inexorably: each disturbing phone call, each disgusting note left in Gail's locker takes the reader along with Gail toward the inevitable attack by a psychotic acquaintance. In fact, the mysterious elements in the novel earned it an Edgar Allan Poe Mystery Award in 1977. And there are some bright spots in the novel: Gail's family is drawn closer together as a result of the rape; Madame Malevich, Gail's colorful drama teacher, is about as helpful as a teacher can be; and Gail comes through it with an insightful determination not to be handicapped by this painful event.

Peck was inspired to write this very popular and honored novel after he received review copies of several nonfiction books about rape, all of which indicated that the most likely rape victim was a teenage girl. But then, Peck says, "each book dropped her like a stone and went on to discuss the victim as a figure in the adult world."[1] And so Peck set out to set the record straight, as he explains:

> I wanted my readers to know some things about this crime, that our laws are stacked against the victim and in favor of the criminal. I wanted them to know some of the medical aspects of this problem, and I also wanted them to know what it's like to be a victim. I had to do a lot of research and interview a lot of people and go to a lot of places. I had to talk to doctors and lawyers and police personnel and victims. I had to deal only in the truth. I couldn't put a happy ending on this story because we don't have any happy endings to this problem in our society.[2]

There were other things that Richard Peck wanted readers to know, he says. He wanted to include a rape crisis center but decided against it because he feared that many readers might not have access to such places. He also wanted to include a courtroom scene but did not write one because, he says, "The typical case is never reported, much less brought to trial."[3]

This novel, the best of the few novels on this topic, accomplishes two other important things. It does not describe the forced intercourse (Gail is knocked unconscious), and it does graphically describe the pelvic examination that follows when Gail is brought to the hospital. Peck explains that he did not want the rape scene to be a "gratuitous horror story," but he did want the pelvic examination to be the most explicit scene in the book. "Research indicated that the typical rape victim never goes for medical treatment and attention. I wanted my readers to know what this treatment is and why it's vital."[4]

Although he had been determined to write the novel, Peck worried that it would ruin his career. However, with the exception of *Kirkus,* reviewers praised it highly, calling it "sensitive, tasteful,"[5] "honest and perceptive,"[6] and "neither sensational nor pornographic."[7] J. W.

Levy, writing in the *Journal of Reading* went so far as to recommend that the novel "be required reading for all teenagers."[8] Librarians of the Young Adult Services Division of the ALA named this one of the "Best of the Best Books 1970–82." Although a feminist reviewer for the *New York Times*, herself a rape victim at age eleven, found the novel too melodramatic and fear-producing, she was honest enough to say that her fifteen-year-old daughter reacted differently, finding the story "edifying and convincing."[9] Students in the Iowa Books for Young Adults program chose it as one of the best books of 1977.[10] And while it has been the combination of students, teachers, and librarians who have made this Richard Peck's best-selling novel, it is the opinion of young people, after all, that counts the most. Interestingly enough, Richard Peck's letters about this book have never included one from a young reader who says she has been raped.

Although *Father Figure* has sold fewer copies than Richard Peck's other novels for young adults, it contains some of his best writing. In fact, Peck views it as his best book, and *Publishers Weekly* in 1978 said it was "assuredly one of the best for all ages in many a moon."[11] Surprisingly it did not make as many "best books" lists as some of Peck's other novels have, although *Booklist* and *School Library Journal* each gave it a starred review, the American Library Association named it a "Best Book for Young Adults" in 1978, and years later the ALA Young Adult Services Division named it one of the "Best of the Best 1970–1982."

Possibly the lack of action in the novel makes it less appealing to teenage readers. This is a quiet, intense book for the most part, though it's not somber, even if it is about how an insecure teenager deals with the death of a parent. Nothing exciting happens, although Jim Atwater, the cynical, reflective main character and narrator, does explode verbally on three occasions. Most of the time, seventeen-year-old Jim maintains a cool exterior as long as he possibly can. On the night before his mother's funeral, for example, Jim says:

> Two nights ago she was sitting strapped in the front seat of the Buick, undiscovered. Last night she was on a marble slab, being drained. Tonight she's under a lid on Madison Avenue. Tomorrow

night she'll be ashes. Even the thing—the disease that was growing
in her—will be ashes. I can cry now in total privacy. So let it happen.
Nothing does.

   Coming to terms with his mother's death is only one of Jim's problems. Jim and his eight-year-old brother Byron have been living with
their uncommunicative, cool maternal grandmother in Brooklyn
Heights since their father abandoned them eight years earlier. From
the time when their mother became incapacitated with her illness,
Jim has assumed responsibility for Byron. Now, suddenly, the two
boys are being sent to Florida to live with their father, a man they
know nothing about, not even what he looks like. Throughout the
summer, Jim attempts to punish his father for past transgressions
while preventing him from becoming the central parental figure in
Byron's life. The conflict provides an unusual twist in the archetypal
coming-of-age plot: in order to grow up, Jim first has to relinquish
his parental role with his younger brother. Once he is able to do that,
he can finish his senior year in high school and make his plans for
college and his life as an adult. In the process, Jim comes to terms
with his father as well, providing an emotional, upbeat finale to
the novel.

   (An excellent analysis of the entire process of how Jim deals with
his emotions—regarding his mother, his brother, his father, his father's girlfriend, and himself—is provided in "The Death of the
Mother, the Rebirth of the Son: *Millie's Boy* and *Father Figure*" by
James T. Henke.[12])

   One of the factors that makes this such an important book is its examination of the father–son relationship, a rarity in books for young
adults. Peck had a strong desire to explore the topic of male emotions
in this novel, a topic he examined further in *Close Enough to Touch*
and *Remembering the Good Times*. In fact, Peck has stated his intent
to "do a body of work" exploring the feelings of boys and men that
will enable them to show their more sensitive side and to communicate with others more effectively.[13]

   At least one parent does not share Peck's concern about the male's
inability to communicate. In "The Genteel Unshelving of a Book,"
Peck explains his surprise at the attitude of the mother of a thirteen-

year-old girl in "a picture-perfect" American town who in 1985 not only refused to allow her daughter to read *Father Figure* but who also succeeded in having the book removed from the junior high school library. For starters, this well-dressed wife of a prominent physician objected to the mother's suicide, then criticized other aspects of the novel that she felt were objectionable: "another book about divorced parents; the angry disrespect of a son for his father; the inability of a parent to shape his child." "'We set a good standard for our daughter, and we don't want to be undermined,'" Peck recalls her saying.[14] For a writer who has criticized parents for not having control over their children, Peck found this kind of parental governance very disturbing.

James Henke proposes a different approach to this novel: "With the aid of sensitive teaching, *Father Figure* can make the young reader understand that the traumas of adolescence are not unique and that the volatile emotions that may be seething inside him are not 'evil' but, rather, logically explicable."[15]

In talking with teenagers and in examining best-seller lists from paperback publishers, Richard Peck learned that love stories are favorites with teenagers. *Close Enough to Touch* was inspired specifically by a seventh-grade boy in a Toronto library who asked, "Say, listen, have you written anything on dating?"[16] "They want love stories? All right, I'll try one, but I won't play their game," Peck decided.[17] First, he wrote it about a boy, and it remains to this day one of the few teenage love stories told from a male's point of view. Second, the story is not about finding the right girl but about, as Peck put it, "that long dry spell between girls."[18] And it's not just about losing a girlfriend; this one left without warning, dying from an aneurysm. Moreover, it's about male emotions, specifically grief, self-pity, loneliness, and the inability to communicate those feelings. Along the way, Peck deals with social-class differences, teenage conformity, and several school-related issues, including what Peck sees as absurd courses like "Contemporary Social Issues" and incompetent teachers who rely on photocopied worksheets to do their teaching for them. Thus, behind the new look of the romance-inspired book cover on *Close Enough to Touch*, it's all vintage Peck. In addition, Peck revealed to a California newspaper reporter, "I suppose there is more of me in Matt than I am willing to admit."[19]

As in *Father Figure*, the father–son relationship is also an important part of *Close Enough to Touch*, even though the novel's main concern is how a teenager copes with the sudden death of his girlfriend. Matt Moran, a high school junior, narrating his own story in the present tense, is a more relaxed, less cynical version of Jim Atwater. Matt's father, a former military man, is sensitive and understanding. Matt's stepmother, Beth, is also sensitive and supportive. Late at night after the funeral of Matt's girlfriend, Dory, Beth tells Matt:

> I'm not anybody's mother. I never have quite figured out who I am. I don't know if we women think we've got a corner on emotions. All I know is, your dad went to bed early tonight because he didn't know what to say to you. And I sat up waiting for you, but I didn't know what to say either.

Touched by her concern, Matt acknowledges his appreciation of Beth for the first time. It's not that he doesn't have emotions—he has more of them than he can handle; he just has trouble expressing them. Later in the story, after Matt gets drunk and cries for the first time, he and his father have an important talk. Matt tells the reader: "Dad always thinks what he has to offer isn't good enough. It's good enough for me." By explaining to his father how much he loved Dory, that they had such great plans for the future, and now there is nothing, Matt feels relieved. His father's clichéd but significant exit line is "A boy needs his dad." And, of course, Matt does.

Supported in his grief by his parents and his energetic grandmother, Matt continues to deal with his self-pity. Intending to spend the rest of the school semester at his family's lakeside cottage, Matt comes across Margaret Chasen—a cocky, candid, nonconformist senior—who has been thrown from her horse. In the process of helping the injured Margaret, he realizes he is attracted to her, and, returning to school, he begins a lengthy process of pursuing her and leaving dead Dory, along with her snobbish, conformist friends, behind. Symbolically, this turning point occurs on Easter weekend. It's not an easy process, to be sure, especially because Matt and Margaret do a lot of verbal sparring. But some of the book's most humorous lines occur during this part of the novel, and the book ends with a quirky, joyful scene.

Unlike *Father Figure*, this novel received a varied response from critics. No one was cool toward it, however. On the enthusiastic side were the *New York Times Book Review, Book Review Digest, Publishers Weekly*, and the *Bulletin of the Center for Children's Books*. The latter called the novel "compelling and bittersweet."[20] Norma Bagnoll in *The ALAN Review* wrote that the story "could have leaned towards the maudlin except for Peck's superb infusion of humor and his emphatic, yet unsentimental, tone."[21] But a Washington librarian reviewer for *School Library Journal* found the narrator's worldly wisdom inconsistent with his immature actions, and labeled the book "predictable."[22] The most cutting attack came from a *Bestsellers* reviewer who called the story "trivial," as well as "shallow and tedious," recommending it only for "light casual reading for some callow freshmen."[23] The American Library Association obviously did not share that opinion, because they listed *Close Enough to Touch* as one of 1981's Best Books for Young Adults. It remains one of the best of the very few books available on the subject of male emotions.

While both *Father Figure* and *Close Enough to Touch* begin with a death and end with the rebirth of the main character, *Remembering the Good Times* does the opposite: it begins with the birth of a foal (in a barn that is later bulldozed out of existence) and ends with the suicide of one of the books' three main characters. The novel filled a serious void in the bibliographies of problem books by examining the symptoms of teenage suicide, a problem of epidemic proportions in contemporary American society, and in the process received more reviews than any other book Peck has written.

There was little disagreement among critics about *Remembering the Good Times*. Except for one critic who foolishly faulted Peck for not providing *the* answer to why teenagers commit suicide,[24] and another who took issue with the way school is portrayed,[25] everyone else praised this novel highly, valuing it for its depth of character development, "finely honed style,"[26] "quiet intensity,"[27] and unsentimental examination of suicide. *Publishers Weekly*, in fact, boxed off its review for emphasis and called the novel Peck's "best book so far."[28] Although Mary Oran, writing in the *Book Report*, predicted that teenagers will neither identify with the characters in this novel nor "stick with this book,"[29] high school students participating in the Iowa Young Adult Book Poll proved her wrong by selecting *Remembering the Good Times* as one of the best books they had read in 1986.[30]

Peck wrote the book in part as the result of student reaction to *Close Enough to Touch*. When he asked teenagers what a boy might do in responding to the kind of loss Matt experienced when his girlfriend Dory dies, Peck was shocked when they answered "kill himself."[31] Hearing the identical response wherever he talked with students across the country, Richard Peck immediately began to research the causes and signs of teenage suicide as the basis for his next novel.

Instead of writing a book that focuses on the suicide itself and how it affects those left behind—as Fran Arrick's *Tunnel Vision* and Susan Beth Pfeffer's *About David* do very effectively—Peck focused instead on the friendship that develops among three young teenagers during a period of nearly four years (much more time than young adult novels usually cover), thus allowing readers not only to become involved with the characters but also to observe the subtle clues that portend one troubled boy's fatal act. In addition, this book is also about several topics that Peck deals with in his other novels: class differences, the suburbanization of rural areas, conformity, the inadequacies of school programs and their administrators, and the importance of caring adults in teenagers' lives.

As in *Father Figure* and *Close Enough to Touch*, the relationship between fathers and sons and the need for boys to express feelings are key elements in this novel. While the bright, self-driven Trav Kirby refuses to communicate with his affluent parents, the less intellectual Buck Mendenhall, who lives with his hard-working father in a trailer at the edge of town, learns to express his emotions. Buck's father, in fact, showing his emotions, tells Buck how he feels about him and later encourages Buck to let out his emotional pain, so that at the end of the book everyone—including a sensitive reader—has a purifying cry.

Buck, who tells this story in retrospect, is an unusual—and refreshing—teenage narrator. He's an excellent observer, but it takes him a while to understand what he sees. As one reviewer analyzed Buck: "His insights never match his observations, . . . and he's neither as clever and charismatic as Kate nor as bright and driven as Trav."[32] Buck, Peck reports, was his third, but wisest, choice for a narrator, since it was inappropriate for Trav to explain his own confused view of the world ("the whole novel would have become a suicide note") and Kate, though she is a wonderfully tough, independent character, would have given the story too strong a touch of romance.

Three other characters enlarge this novel, making it more entertaining and insightful. The first is Skeeter Calhoon, the psychopathic bully who harasses not only Buck but also a first-year English teacher. Trav sees a lot of his own anger and confusion in Skeeter but realizes that "Skeeter acts out all his aggressions, and I just keep mine in and let them eat at me." Second is Sherrie Slater, the new English teacher, who is hopelessly unprepared to deal with junior high kids, especially without a supportive school administration. She becomes Peck's most extreme vehicle for criticizing the American educational system. And Polly Prior, Kate's great-grandmother—a balding, cranky, wheelchair-bound old lady who cheats at cards— provides snatches of wisdom as well as a significant link to the past that helps make this novel so vibrant. Polly's pear orchard also provides a symbolic link to the past, a past that is being wiped out by spreading subdivisions and shopping malls. The inevitability of this incursion helps to drive Trav to hang himself from a branch of one of those trees. Memorable characters all. "In fact," a *Los Angeles Times* reviewer wrote, "all the characters shimmer."[33]

9. Satire and Beyond

Published exactly midway between his four problem novels, *Secrets of the Shopping Mall* is unlike any of Richard Peck's other works. It has won no prizes, made no one's "best books" list. Yet it engendered more reviews than all but one of his other novels, and almost all of the reviewers made negative remarks. It also is his least well crafted novel. But it results in more letters to the author than any of his other novels, and it has out sold most of Peck's books that did make best books lists. Like a movie that receives no Academy Award nominations but outsells every other film of the year at the box office, *Secrets of the Shopping Mall* is not an impressive literary work but younger teenagers seem to love it, though not for the reasons that Peck wrote it.

What makes this novel unusual are its setting and its concept, which are almost the same in this case. The concept is a brilliant one, the reasoning behind it perfectly logical: today's climate-controlled shopping malls contain everything to sustain life. Many contemporary teenagers use their local mall as the focal point in their lives, going there after school or, as Peck says, often instead of school. If not ordered to leave at closing time, a person could live inside a mall indefinitely—if he or she hid somewhere until the security guards left. That's exactly what Peck's characters do. A "nutty premise" Patty Campbell called it, but an "especially delicious" one.[1]

Escaping from the vicious King Kobra gang at their chaotic, graffiti-covered inner-city junior high school, loners Teresa and Barnie spend their last two dollars on bus fare to Paradise Park, New Jersey, where they hide out in a large department store. Sleeping beneath the beds in the Beds and Bedding department by day and roaming the darkened store by night, they feed themselves from the refrigerated deli unit in the Gourmet department and "borrow" new clothing from whatever department suits their fancy. Their families won't miss them because thirteen-year-old Teresa lives with an aunt who doesn't care and Barnie—"too smart for the seventh grade and too short for the eighth"—lives in a foster home that probably won't even report him missing. In the mall they at last feel safe. Besides, there is no school to attend, no adult to set limits for them—in fact, no one to tell them what to do. So they think.

They find out otherwise. The store is filled with other runaway teenagers like themselves, though the others are from permissive, affluent, suburban homes. Like Teresa and Barnie, they roam the store by night, wearing the latest name-brand fashions, and hide by day, often "freezing" like a store mannequin. Their names identify the departments over which they watch: Swank from Cuff Links, Crystal from Stemware, etc. They are ruled by the beautiful blond Barbie and the immaculately dressed preppie Ken, who look "like an advertisement for a modeling school." They all go along with the dictatorial Barbie because it's easier than thinking for themselves. What they have done is exchange one type of gang at school for a different one at the mall, one type of authority figure at home for an even worse one at the mall.

To make matters even worse, the group inside the mall is attacked by the Mouth-Breathers—the black leather jacket gang that rules the parking lot around the mall. But the resourceful Teresa finds a way to stop the melee and preserve their turf.

Being independent thinkers, Teresa and Barnie also wrangle themselves legitimate jobs in the department store, then rally some members of the group to rebel against Barbie's dictatorial decisions, after which all the kids decide to go back home while Teresa and Barnie stay on to enjoy their new productive lives.

"A bizarre farce," one reviewer called it.[2] An "offbeat comedy/

mystery/fantasy ... too frantic, and occasionally confusing," another one wrote.[3] *Kirkus* labeled it a "ham-handed satire."[4] The *English Journal* reviewers wrote: "What Peck was probably aiming for was the ultimate satire on suburbia, but unfortunately where he landed is somewhere beyond realism but short of fantasy."[5]

Whatever its label, Peck says he intended the story as "a commentary on being young in the 1980s, an age in which the young no longer go from home to school, but go from the TV set to the shopping mall."[6] "And I wrote it as a satire, with these kids as pioneers on the last American frontier."[7] *Time* magazine called it " 'Lord & Taylor of the Flies.' "[8]

His first version of the novel was too negative, with everybody getting "what he deserved in the end." But two years later he rewrote it in a lighter vein, hoping that kids could laugh at themselves. "I had learned already that when you write for teenagers, you can only tell them so much bad news, unless it's about somebody's mother."[9] But young readers don't necessarily read the book the way Peck intended it. For one thing, a number of readers—adults as well as teenagers— misinterpret part of the action. Because Teresa and Barnie at first think the mannequins have come alive, some readers interpret the story as science fiction. In addition, many young readers don't see the point that these kids have given up one gang for another, one kind of tyranny for another. They don't see that "it can still be a gang even if they're well-dressed and the girls are picture-perfect models. They don't get that; they don't want to."

Nevertheless, some of Peck's usual themes are sure to come through to some readers: the need to act independently and not blindly follow the leader of a group, the importance of genuine friendship, being an outsider, the inability of educators to educate kids, and the emphasis on designer labels in our society. And even if readers don't "get it," they can have fun fantasizing a life in their own mall while their letters urge Richard Peck to write a sequel. In this age of series books, Peck says: "There ought to be a series called Mall Rats. I'm not happy with that setting, but . . . ."

Both of Richard Peck's most recent novels—his fourteenth and fifteenth for young adults—are not as easily categorized as their predecessors. *Princess Ashley* is part problem novel, part romance.

It's about peer pressure and conformity; parent–child relationships and the lack of adult control; and school and friendship and alcoholism and self-concept. *Those Summer Girls I Never Met* deals with the relationships between brothers and sisters, between children and parents, and between young people and old people, while it examines nostalgic elements from the past. It also deals with facing death and with male emotions. On top of it all, it's Peck's funniest novel excepting the Blossom Culp books.

The themes in *Princess Ashley*—conformity and parent–child relationships—are vintage Peck. But they are not just part of the story, as they are in his previous novels; here they *are* the story. Peck is his most direct in this novel; no teenage reader can possibly miss the point that it's unwise to follow a self-appointed leader blindly; no adult reader can possibly miss the point that it's unwise for parents to pamper their children and give up control with the hope that kids will do the right things on their own. Adults play a large role in this novel, especially the narrator's mother, who becomes the spokesperson for much of Peck's philosophy. At the end of the novel, Mrs. Olinger—ironically, a school guidance counselor—says to her daughter: "'I've been too much like any other parent, and you've been too much like any other child. We give you all this space and time, and you do nothing with it but damage.'"

The danger in this approach, of course, is that the novel become didactic. Peck is sometimes a little heavy-handed, for example when his sixteen-year-old narrator says, "At fourteen you can believe anything you want," or "in tenth grade you like rumors better than the truth anyway." But for the most part, the action illustrates clearly enough that the teenagers are out of control. They reach a crisis point in the middle of the novel when Gloria, the school's most volatile female student, smashes Mrs. Olinger in the face with a metal wastebasket, and again at the climax of the novel when Craig, the school's most out-of-control male student, crashes his classy sports car after drinking irresponsibly. Thus, it is easy to accept the adults' advice to their children, because the book's previous events enable the reader to see how right the adults are. In a hospital bed after Gloria's attack on her, Mrs. Olinger tells her daughter Chelsea, "I guess she was just—overcome with anger at the whole adult world for letting her be what she is. And she knew she could get away with it. . . . It's scary when you know you won't be held responsible, for anything. Your whole generation seems to be having that problem." Even though Chelsea doesn't yet understand the implications of what her mother has told her, readers ought to. And when Craig's father says, "When we couldn't control him, we just hoped for the best," readers can see their regret and their grief because by then Craig is lying brain-damaged and paralyzed in the hospital.

What also makes this novel work so well is Peck's choice of narrator. Instead of being a perceptive interpreter of life, as many narrators of young adult novels are, Chelsea has a serious blind spot: she's an insecure teenager who wants to belong in her new school, and so she doesn't comprehend what she's doing or why. Being a typical teenager, she also wants no contact with her parents. In the opening scene of the novel she even sits scrunched against the door on the passenger side of the car, as far away from her mother as she can get in their old Dodge as they drive to their new home. She also demands that her mother keep her own identity separate from Chelsea's at school. Once school starts, Chelsea blindly follows the manipulative Ashley Packard who had "been in charge from the first day she set foot in the sandbox." Chelsea doesn't see her misjudgments until two hundred pages, two years, and two tragedies later. It's an effective technique, masterfully executed.

This harsh look at teenage life reflects Peck at his angriest. "It's my toughest novel," Peck admits.[10] He has said, "I think the real fuel for all writing is anger." When asked if he feels angrier now than when he first started writing, Peck's unhesitating reply was "Oh, infinitely." Writing about *Princess Ashley* in her master's thesis on Richard Peck, Janice K. Tovey concludes: "After numerous novels in which he asked questions of [readers], he seems to want to shock them into questioning their own values and attitudes. He seems less tolerant of their attention to their peers and angry that they relinquish their own identity."[11]

This novel, however, is not all serious, for Peck knows very well that teenage readers want to be entertained when they read. In fact, there is a lot of humor in this novel, and the most reliable source of it is Pod Johnson, an insightful, oddball student who, though bright and rich, projects the image of a bumpkin. His efforts at writing poetry in English class alone are enough to make him memorable. Pod, the *Los Angeles Times* wrote, is "one of the most winning characters in young adult fiction."[12]

In addition to high praise from various reviewers, such as *Kirkus*, which singled out Peck's "unusual wisdom and empathy for the teen condition,"[13] *Princess Ashley* received *VOYA's* highest possible rating for quality and popularity[14]—and was named one of 1987's best books by the American Library Association as well as *School Library Journal*. Teenage readers in Colorado also nominated it for the Blue Spruce Young Adult Book Award for 1988.

Humor dominates *Those Summer Girls I Never Met*, though sorrowful situations lurk behind the exterior summer adventures of two teenagers. Drew (for Andrew) Wingate, who is just weeks away from being sixteen years old and expecting to have the summer of his life as soon as he gets his driver's license, has a colorful view of the world and a talent for describing it with exceptional wit. For example, he describes his fourteen-year-old sister Stephanie: "Steph's the all-suburban champion door banger for her weight and class. She practices." She also spends a lot of time in her room, "with her Walkman in one ear and her Trimline in the other and a VCR running." Like a typical teenager, she tries to avoid being with adults. "Eating with her nearest relatives kills her appetite. Her room smells like a deli, and she does a lot of feeding straight from the refrigerator, off-hours." She, of course, finds Drew as obnoxious as he finds her, and that makes their mother's announcement even more horrifying: instead of the summer they are dreaming about, they will be spending two weeks on a cruise ship leaving from England with their sixty-four-year-old grandmother, whom they haven't seen in ten years. Drew remarks: "At our age, if there's one thing you don't want to see, it's the world."

Their grandmother turns out to be Connie Carlson, a vivacious jazz singer from the forties—"the Madonna of her particular generation"—who is on this cruise to entertain the mainly elderly passengers in the ship's nightclub. "She can make an audience of people just her age be young again, and in love with each other," one of the ship's entertainers says. She's also there to get acquainted with her two grandchildren before it's too late, for she has a secret that the kids discover as they visit Copenhagen, Leningrad, Helsinki, Stockholm, and Oslo. One of Drew's greatest adventures during the trip is meeting Holly, the ship's dance instructor. She's a gorgeous twenty-two, and trying his best to look as old as possible, he pursues her lustfully, a task that often has amusing results.

In the process, both Drew and his sister mature, come to love their bizarre grandmother, find out something about their previously unaccounted-for grandfather, get to understand their mother a little better, see a bit of Europe, and tune in to music from an age they once thought was prehistoric. There is also an emotional scene during which one of the families on the ship encounters the grandmother in Russia whom they had previously been unable to contact, thus providing a lesson for today's American teenagers who take much for granted. Peck skillfully uses his own experiences working on a cruise ship, his knowledge of foreign cities, and his nostalgic feelings for the past and blends them with some of his most common young adult themes—relationships between young and old, taking independent action, and viewing the world from a wider perspective—to produce a novel that is both funny and sad, instructs without being didactic, and is, above all, uplifting.

10. Adult Novels

"You could write a historical novel like Rosemary Rogers," Richard Peck recalls his editor at Avon saying one day. Peck had already written half a dozen novels for teenagers with no thought about writing any other kind. He was familiar with teenagers because of his frequent contacts with them, but he knew little about the type of adults who would be the audience for the kind of book his editor was suggesting. Peck's immediate reply was, "No, I couldn't." "Yes, you could," the editor insisted.

Switching tactics, the editor said, "*If* you were going to, where would you set it?" The answer came rather quickly from Peck, "I'd set it in the Edwardian Era, which is accessible, and around everybody's favorite disaster, the sinking of the *Titanic*." She said, "Fine, I'll draw up a contract. Get going." And the rest, to twist a common expression, is historical fiction.

Because Peck likes nonfiction and enjoys doing historical research, and because England is one of his favorite places, the setting and the background for his first adult novel were ideally suited to him. For the place, Peck chose the Isle of Wight, on which he had once vacationed. "I had walked all over it," he recounts. "The Isle of Wight is a wonderful setting because it's England in microcosm. It has one castle, one royal palace, one this, one that . . ." He also joined the Titanic Historical Society of America, studied the histories of families who were on the ship, and, he says, "lived for two years with the deck plan of the Titanic around my room." Because so many people are well versed in *Titanic* lore, Peck felt that he needed to be absolutely accurate about the locations of everything on board, to the point of knowing which way his characters would turn when they left their staterooms.

Because he also was working on other projects, his first book for adults took him more than four years to complete, and he was not comfortable writing it. But *Amanda/Miranda* attained phenomenal success in spite of one critic's contention that "The implausibility of the story" made the novel "hardly food for the serious older reader."[1] Avon's initial intent was to publish the novel in an original paperback format, but they wisely decided to let Viking Press release it in hardcover first. "[E]verything you could hope would happen to a book happened to *Amanda/Miranda*," Peck told interviewer Jean Ross.[2] It was translated into nine languages and printed in special editions by the Literary Guild and Reader's Digest, as well as in Braille. Although the book is now out of print, it continues to be a popular choice in libraries. (This writer had to get on a waiting list to borrow the book from the West Hartford Public Library seven years after the book was first published!) And Richard Peck received, and still receives, a hefty volume of letters about the book—this time from adult readers. Encouraged by the discovery of this new audience in 1980, he then wrote two more novels for adults.

A reader of *Amanda/Miranda* cannot fail to be reminded of "Upstairs/Downstairs," with its blushing chambermaids, colorful kitchen crew, and veddy veddy rich owners of the estate. But there are twists in Peck's tale of romance, intrigue, deception, and adventure. Although a reviewer for the *Washington Post* thought the book a "jumbled hand-me-down from Mishmasterpiece Theatre," others found it to be "a gorgeously romantic, implausible affair comfy as eiderdown"[3] and "A wry . . . portrait of Edwardian social manners, . . . written with a subtlety and vigor of style that are a continual delight."[4]

The tale focuses on Amanda—the selfish, overindulged, devious daughter of the owners of Whitwell Hall—and her new, innocent servant, Mary, renamed Miranda by Amanda, after the heroine in Shakespeare's *The Tempest*. Among the cast in the manor are John Thorne, the estate's maintenance man and chauffeur who is also Amanda's secret lover; Gregory Forrest, the handsome, idealistic American son of a German beer baron who is courting Amanda; Amanda's black-sheep brother, Gordon; along with Mrs. Creeth, "the cook and empress of the kitchen"; Mr. Finley, "the Butler above and dictator below"; and various other rich folks and their servants. It just so happens that Amanda and Miranda are look-alikes, thus establishing the possibilities for mistaken identities and intermixed romances—Amanda and Thorne, Amanda and Gregory, Miranda and Thorne, and Miranda and Gregory.

Amanda sums up her own character: "I am meant to have what I want." And she sets elaborate schemes to do that, including making Miranda "a mirror of herself" and arranging for John Thorne and Miranda to marry. Poor Miranda is victimized not only by Amanda but also by John Thorne and by life in general in this high society. Her mother, she says, "taught me subservience but not survival." But Miranda is not stupid, and she learns from each painful episode. "I had been raised to expect nothing for myself," she explains, but little by little she nurtures small sparks of self-worth and independence within herself until she eventually vows to be "no one's easy convenience ever again."

Her chance for independence comes late in the novel, during her crossing to America on board the *Titanic* with Amanda. Amanda— secretly pregnant with Thorne's baby, though Thorne is conveniently now married to Miranda and Amanda is on her way to marry Gregory—drowns in the sinking, while Miranda, dressed like Amanda and wearing Amanda's jewelry, is rescued from the icy waters. In love with Gregory since she first met him, Miranda, masquerading now as Amanda, becomes a bigamist by marrying Gregory and finds happiness in America.

Much more than a stereotypical historical romance, this novel clearly delineates the manners of the times and elucidates the attitudes of the upper class toward servants and of servants toward their masters and mistresses. It is also the story of strong women, especially of a woman who gains strength in herself as she loses her innocence. It was Peck's intent to reverse the usual role of women in romance novels where they are the prizes for strong men. "I have presented the heroine as the ingenious one in adversity, winner of the male prize, for a change," he told a *Publishers Weekly* interviewer. "I also made up my mind to do in the story what I try to do in novels for young people: give readers leading characters they can look up to and reasons to believe that problems can be solved."[5]

In addition, although reviewer Jane Langton found only the details of the sinking of the *Titanic* "authentic,"[6] the novel is chock full of vivid details about clothing, architecture, transportation, and daily life of the Edwardian Age. For example, in Chapter 8, Peck describes some of what young Miranda sees throughout Whitwell Hall:

> The Flemish tapestries set in the bleached and silvered panels. The infinity of mirrors set up by the thousand curving silversides of teapots and urns high on their tripods. The morning room a garden of subtly shaded chintz flowers covering the graceful curves of the chair backs. The great glittering chandeliers.

Later there are detailed descriptions of the Russian-inspired ladies' fashions popular in London in the early 1900s. The sense of place remains with the reader long after the details of the story have faded.

And people did respond to the story. Many of them were in their seventies and eighties. Some were family members of people who had been on the *Titanic*, wanting to know if Peck had known their relatives, assuming of course that he could not have written about the event so vividly without having experienced it firsthand. One woman from Altadena, California, has written to him weekly since the book came out. She is almost ninety years old now. Along the way, she sent Peck some documents her mother had recorded at her job in a Pasadena library, among them a young woman's account of traveling west in a covered wagon in the mid-1800s. That account inspired and formed the basis for Peck's third adult novel, *This Family of Women*, which he dedicated to his faithful correspondent: Isabelle Daniels Griffis.

Although Peck wrote *Amanda/Miranda* for an adult audience, some reviewers believe the book is appropriate for teenagers as well.

One of those is Joni Bodart, who argued that *Amanda/Miranda* should have been on the ALA Best Books for Young Adults list for 1980.[7] Certainly older teens, especially females, will find the novel of interest. Peck wryly observes about his two constituencies: "It's wonderful, but it makes you realize that you are in two fields in which you are just about to lose your readers: teenagers grow up very quickly and the very old die."[8] To deal with that problem, Richard Peck decided to write a novel for people his own age who are going through midlife crises.

New York Time grew out of a comment from one of Richard Peck's friends— "a woman younger than I by a generation"—who, Peck recalls, complained: "'There are no novels about me.'" She had gone to college, joined a sorority, and married the guy most likely to succeed. "[She] now lives in a dream house in Winnetka, and has come to the time in her life when she says, 'So is this it?'"

"Marriages are funny things," thirty-eight-year-old Barbara Renfrew says in the opening line of *New York Time*. "Let me tell you about mine." What she reveals in this witty, satirical novel is that she's "quietly confused." Not only does she miss the romance of her college sorority days, but also her once secure life with husband Tom in a Chicago suburb is disrupted when he is transferred to New York City. They leave behind people like themselves, such as their neighbor Libby—"She's Supermom, and a full-time scourge of the PTA"— and their "neo-Georgian [house] with double door beneath beaded fanlight. Williamsburg high-gloss enamel trim with brass lion's mask knocker winking in the gray day."

Barbara finds New York impossible to cope with. Apartment-hunting in Manhattan is horrifying (a dead body recently decorated the floor of the apartment they eventually lease). Anyone who has ever been the least bit confounded or fearful or lost or frustrated in the Big Apple will recognize and sympathize with Barbara's emotions. The WASP from middle-class middle-America has a hard time adjusting. And then Tom leaves her, wants a divorce, goes back to the North Shore of Chicago to an old flame, Marlene Millsap (the name tells it all).

Barbara falls apart, leading an empty, aimless life sustained by soap operas, until she meets Ed, an urban horticulturalist. He's twenty-three, tall, handsome, sexy, and gentle with her. Twenty-three! Their passion triumphs over everything else. He makes her very happy. Then he makes her pregnant, which makes her even happier. And of course he asks Barbara to marry him.

Unhappy with Marlene, Tom returns to beg Barbara to take him back. But she's found herself and her love and her place in the world and so she sends Tom away. She marries Ed. Tom marries Marlene. And Ed's great-grandmother dies and leaves them her enormous, gorgeous apartment. The end.

A reviewer from the Boston Public Library was right on target drawing a comparison between Erma Bombeck's style and Barbara's skewed views of life's vagaries.[9] But not everyone appreciates Erma Bombeck's kind of humor. Thus Peck came in for his share of negative comments on this book. One reviewer did not like the abundance of "aphorisms and digressions" but found them "undeniably witty" and the ending "moving."[10] *Kirkus* found the ending "saccharine" and the book as a whole without sufficient impact, even though it contains "lots of fine witchy humor."[11] An Ohio librarian wondered "why any man would be attracted to Peck's listless heroine."[12] And Stoddard Martin, writing in the *Times Literary Supplement* skewered the entire presentation with: "This book was written for Madison Avenue: it has the sheen and wit of the best advertising prose, and pushes the same optimistic humbug."[13]

The reviewer for *Booklist*, focusing on what others had minimized, praised the "memorable eccentricities and abundant zesty barbs, well and liberally planted."[14] But the reviewer for *Mademoiselle* seems to have understood the novel best, saying that *New York Time* "is not profound and doesn't pretend to be." She labeled it "amusing" and "urbane," "a shrewd and witty modern version of a 1940s movie."[15]

Peck's intent, he says, was to examine "the mid-life crises of men and women of the educated middle class," but the only way to do that was as a comedy, "because it hurts too much otherwise."[16] Peck acknowledges that Ed is too good to be true; but "everybody knows Tom," Peck says. Although it's clearly a book for women, Peck received a lot of letters from men. They write about the kinds of experiences they have had in New York: "the crazy people on the subway, trying to find an apartment in New York. . . . But it's also a very warm response that 'We've been through this together, haven't we?' . . . Or 'You can't fool me—you went to my college.'" That's the kind of response Peck values most. And because of that kind of response, *New York Time* is Peck's "sentimental favorite" novel.

This Family of Women is awash with interesting characters—mostly female—and the stories of the real women behind the fictional characters are just as interesting. Peck explains the theory behind his lengthy saga:

> [T]he American West was not won by men with guns but by women without them. When you learn the local histories of towns like Reno and Virginia City, you find that the men were shooting everything in sight, and the women were trying to found the schools and the church and finally the country club. And so I decided to write a western novel in which the real groundbreakers were women instead of men. And each one of the women in my novel is a real woman whose life I fictionalize.[17]

Among the documents sent to Peck by Isabelle Griffis were notes from the diary of Susan Thompson. Her family, traveling to California in 1851, had come upon a tragedy: Indians had killed the adults in the Oatman family, which had been traveling alone just ahead of them, had abducted the teenage daughters, and had scalped and left the son, Lorenzo, to die. Lorenzo survived and he and the Thompsons eventually reached California and settled in El Monte. Years later, Lorenzo located his sister Olive, who had been living with Mohave Indians in Arizona, and brought her back to El Monte. But according to the diary, Olive apparently was unable to adjust to living among whites. To fill in the gaps in Susan Thompson's account and to imagine what might have happened to her, Richard Peck began *This Family of Women*.[18]

From over two years of research, primarily in Carson City, Nevada, and in San Francisco, Richard Peck shaped an epic novel about five generations of women, all related by blood or friendship, starting with fourteen-year-old Lena Wheatley (based on Susan Thompson) and Sarah Ann Ransom (based on Olive Oatman). Book 1 recreates the horrifying events of the wagon trip west. In California, with both

parents dead, Lena marries Evan Freeman. When Sarah Ann is re-
patriated from the Indians, she is found to be pregnant. Her brother
Lorenzo leaves in humiliation to fight for the North in the Civil War.
Lena and Evan raise the mixed race baby, Effie, along with their own
daughter, Opal. Book 2 is Effie's story. She was raised to think Lena
is her mother, though Lena is always cool toward her. They move to
Virginia City where Evan is searching for gold. After Evan's death in
the desert, the women struggle to make ends meet by working in a
boarding house until the great fire of 1875 levels most of the city.
Aiming high, Lena borrows money and builds a classy brothel. Ap-
palled by her mother's act, fifteen-year-old Opal marries and moves
to San Francisco with her husband, Terrance Kinsella. Lorenzo
chances to visit the brothel and Effie falls in love with him, only later
learning that he is her uncle and Sarah Ann is her mother.

As Constance Nichols tells her story in Book 3, she reveals that
she is the daughter of Eve Waring and Anton Nichols, San Francisco
theater people. Anton had changed his wife's name to Eve Waring
and helped make her a famous actress; her former name was Effie.
Eve, believing that "women are only valued for how they look or for
the work they can do," wants "to be valued for who I am." She goes on
to become, as her grandson later says, "the great beauty of the age."
Connie, thinking herself "the ordinary child of . . . extraordinary
parents," has plans to become an architect. Through these fictional
characters the reader is introduced to numerous historical characters, most of them British since the story follows Eve to the society
world of London. Included are Lady Randolph Churchill and her
elder son Winston, George Bernard Shaw, Ethel Barrymore, Lillie
Langtree, Kaiser Wilhelm, and the Prince of Wales (who becomes
Eve's lover). Connie returns to America and later becomes one of the
country's first female architects.

Books 4 and 5 explore the lives of Constance's childhood friend
Rose who becomes a prosperous businesswoman in San Francisco
and Rose's daughter June, who works as a nurse in London during
World War I where she falls in love with Andy Drummond, an air
force pilot who also happens to be Connie's son. Later, almost all of
these characters are involved in some way in the great earthquake
and fire that destroy most of San Francisco in 1906.

The final book, unlike the previous five, is told from a male perspective. Andy recounts Connie's architectural successes, Rose's business accomplishments, June's death in the bombing of London, and Eve's final revelations about her life. As World War II is developing in Europe, it becomes Andy's responsibility to take his daughter Claire away from London to the safety of America. For the first time in this novel a *man* is going to have to keep the family together, to be the nurturer. In Claire he sees not only the beauty she has inherited from Eve, but also "the beginnings of command" and "the assurance to carry her into uncharted territory." And in the final line in the book, Claire leads her father "into the future."

Having begun on grim notes, the novel's ending provides promise and hope for the future of this family of women as well as for female readers of the novel. The women throughout this lengthy book have been made strong through grief and adversity. Most of the men in their lives either abandoned them—as Lorenzo did to his sister and Evan does to Sarah Ann and their children; abused them horribly—as Rose's husband did; or died—as did Lena's father and then her husband, and Connie's father as well as her first love, Hugh. The book, in fact, is replete with negative comments about the behavior of men: "I knew he'd leave us behind because that's what men do." "Men are slow to see." "I was loud with him, and he slunk off as men do." "You expect to be forgiven. Men think that's their right, don't they?"

Not that the women come off looking saintly. The women in the novel often reject others in order to protect themselves. Early in Book 1 Lena says, "I must learn to hold something of myself back, from everyone." Sarah Ann is unable to provide her foster daughter Effie with the love and closeness Effie needs. Effie, as Eve, in turn is unable to give Constance much warmth until her later years, when she admits: "I'd been deprived of love, and so I deprived Constance. We always withhold what was withheld from us. We cannot even see this cycle, let alone find a way to break it." The novel thus addresses a contemporary problem of communication between mothers and daughters in a historical setting.

In addition to having begun the novel from a sketch of real people in a real event, Peck modeled several of the main characters on real women. Vivacious Eve, for instance, was based largely on the American actress Maxine Elliot, "the most beautiful woman who *ever* lived." "She didn't care about riches; she didn't care about clothes; she didn't care about men. She cared about British society." Peck says she is mentioned in "virtually every memoir of a prominent personage, from Edward VII to Noel Coward," and is most clearly delineated in *My Aunt Maxine* by Jean Forbes-Robertson (Viking Press). The Virignia City portion of the novel was inspired by the real-life Isobel Field as described in her autobiography *This Life I've Loved* (circa 1936). Isobel's stepfather was the famous writer Robert Louis Stevenson, with whom her brother Lloyd Osbourne co-authored "The Wrong Box." And the real-life Julia Morgan provided the background for the character of Constance. Julia Morgan, the first female to study architecture at the Ecole des Beaux-Arts in Paris and the first female to receive an architectural degree from the University of California at Berkeley, went on from the beginning of the twentieth century to her death in 1957 to design nearly 800 buildings in a variety of styles, along the way replacing Stanford White as the architect for the rebuilding of the Fairmont Hotel on Nob Hill after the 1906 San Francisco earthquake. Her crowning achievement was the design for San Simeon, William Randolph Hearst's magnificent California mansion, where "she lived out her own medieval fantasy, creating a community of craftsmen, woodcarvers, stone casters, weavers and ironworkers."[19]

After his novel was published, Peck found out what happened to the real Olive Oatman. While speaking to a group of librarians in Los Angeles, he learned that the Oatmans were a prominent family in the area and that the Olive whom he had supposed never readjusted to "civilized" life had, to his embarrassment, become a public speaker, telling people about her life in captivity, and had written a best-selling book!

This Family of Women became a best-seller also, and was a Literary Guild and a Doubleday Book Club alternate selection. Reviewers rightly praised its dramatic impact, its "narrative sweep rich in historic detail,"[20] and its focus on individual women with pasts as well as presents. But several reviewers also justifiably found parts of the book contrived; one found the dialogue and narration in book 1 jar-

ring, though she also felt those elements improve as the book progresses and the narrators become better educated.[21] The most balanced assessment of the novel came from Stephanie Zvirin, writing
in *Booklist*, who contends that even though Peck sometimes leaves
the lives of the characters "maddeningly unsettled, rushing on too
quickly from one generation or narrator to the next," the novel is
nevertheless filled with "historical richness and craftsmanship, and
it rises well above the sweltering passions and cardboard conventions
of so many multigenerational family sagas."[22]

   Although this novel, like *Amanda/Miranda*, was intended for an
adult audience, there is much in it for older teenagers. For one thing,
the rich historical details—from the character of young Winston
Churchill to the architecture of the Fairmont Hotel, from the actions
of Buffalo Bill's Wild West show to the destruction of San Francisco—provide more lasting impressions than do school history
texts. For another, almost all of the major characters are teenage
girls at the start of their story, and each tale is essentially a coming-
of-age story developed over a longer time period than the typical
young adult novel manages. In addition, the shifting of narrators and
the abundance of action keep the 414-page novel moving. The novel,
in fact, was praised for just those characteristics when it was rated as
one of the best books of the year by high school students in the annual Iowa Books for Young Adults Poll.[23]

11. Short Stories and Children's Books

"There are some writers who write one novel after another and for whom any interruption would be anathema. But I'm always looking for materials to use with kids, because I'm still a teacher." And so Richard Peck, usually working in some other form after finishing one of his novels, finds that short stories are a natural for junior and senior high school readers, even though until recently there have been few places in which to publish them. He has published two very successful short stories for a teenage audience: "Priscilla and the Wimps" and "Shadows," and wrote a third in 1988, entitled "I Go Along," which is awaiting publication.

"Priscilla and the Wimps," included in *Sixteen: Short Stories by Outstanding Writers for Young Adults*, has become one of the favorite stories in that collection, praised highly by teenagers as well as by teachers and librarians. Based on characters in the King Kobra gang from Peck's *Secrets of the Shopping Mall*, this very brief story, as one high school reader put it, "is about how bullies get it stuck to them after they push some people too far."[1] In Monk Klutter's case, his comeuppance is provided by a *girl*, Priscilla Roseberry. Although some boys have not been too pleased that a girl gets the better of a boy, young readers in general appreciate not only the fact that Monk is overpowered but especially the manner in which he meets his end.

Reviewer Patty Campbell called this story a "delicious anecdote . . . in which every word builds with exquisite skill to an explosively comical conclusion."[2]

It is no surprise then that another Peck short story leads off a second collection of original stories for young adults published in 1987. In "Shadows," a young woman explains how she had grown up with ghosts in a New Orleans house owned by two eccentric aunts who are her guardians. Rather than fearing them, she says, "Ghosts were the company I came to count on." And then a strange boy appears to her, learns to trust her, learns from her, and grows as she matures . . . until she outgrows him. Years later, as she is preparing to leave for college, he returns for one last time. In critiquing *Visions*, a *VOYA* reviewer concludes that "Shadows" reveals "a different Peck" and notes that his "haunting imagery is enveloped in a beautiful ethereal veil."[3] Peck himself might find the idea of an "ethereal veil" a bit hyperbolic, but the imagery in this short story is certainly vivid and haunting.

In "I Go Along," the male narrator and his peers in a regular eleventh-grade English class wonder why Mrs. Tibbetts is taking her Advanced English class to hear a poet read from his works at a local college but hasn't asked them. Invited to accompany the group, Gene finds himself in unfamiliar territory, first with a girl who sits with him and then with the poet—who doesn't look like what he has imagined a poet to look like and whose poems don't sound like those he's used to reading in school. Both Gene and the reader learn something about poetry in this delightful story that includes two original poems that Peck wrote for the occasion.

It should also be noted that because of their brevity, subject matter, and vivid imagery, all three of these short stories are excellent choices for oral reading by an accomplished reader or storyteller.

Peck demonstrates a more sophisticated writing style in "The Size of the Universe," a short story included in a 1986 issue of the *Southwest Review*. Compared to Peck's young adult stories and novels, the going is heavier here, the images more densely packed. The delineation of character and details of time and place dominate an almost nonexistent plot. As in so much of Peck's writing, physical details are realistic and authentic: from the Studebaker in the driveway and the snowball bushes beside the house to the black-and-white Philco television in the living room and the Electrolux vacuum cleaner in the closet. Although much of this story is from the perspective of a young girl, it is told in the voice of that girl grown into a woman, as she tries to come to terms with a grandmother who dominated the lives of everyone around her. But unlike the rest of Peck's fiction, the ending here is not a hopeful one, though it is certainly one that is in keeping with the kinds of stories one finds in small, sophisticated publications of this kind.

Although Richard Peck has written two books for children, only one has so far been published. Taking a break after completing one of his earlier novels for young adults, Peck thought he'd try writing a story for children, "just to see if I could do it." George Nicholson, then at Viking, liked it and asked Peck whom he would like to illustrate it. "Well, if I could have anybody, I'd have Don Freeman, of course." It took another two years before Freeman finished his share of the book. Soon afterwards, the illustrator died suddenly at a dinner party in New York City.

Monster Night at Grandma's House is a thirty-page story about young Toby's visit to his grandmother's old house in the country where daytime is fun but nighttime is scary. In fact, on this night Toby is sure there's a monster standing near his bed. Opening his eyes and finding no monster, but thinking he sees the end of a tail exiting his doorway, Toby figures the monster is scared of him. Following the monster's trail down the stairs and out onto the porch to make sure it does not return, he falls asleep in the porch swing. In the morning he proudly assures his grandmother that "It's gone. I took care of it. There's not a thing in the world to worry about." A happy ending to a frightening night in which Toby learns to conquer his fears.

The mood of the old Victorian country house with its shadowy hallways, squeaky floorboards, and pesky beetles tapping at the window screens is darkly portrayed by Don Freeman's India ink illustrations on scratchboard with blue watercolor overlays.

The reviewer for *Kirkus* wasn't frightened by it, though, feeling a lack of emotional involvement because "Peck doesn't make [readers] share the terrors."[4] And a Pennsylvania school librarian found the ending a "let down in a wordy and wholly unconvincing tale."[5] But the reviewer in *Language Arts* labeled it an "amusing" and "suspenseful" story that "reads well silently or aloud."[6] And *Publishers Weekly* praised its "reassuring end" and declared that "Every little kid who has ever feared the dark will empathize with Toby."[7] The book's value lies in the switch in Toby's perspective from understandable fearfulness to proud self-assuredness, illustrating once again Richard Peck's desire to leave readers hopeful and stronger at the end.

If his second book for children is ever published, it will probably be called *What Ever Happened to Thanksgiving?* It evolved from a conversation with an Indiana librarian who was also a storyteller. She was content with the number of Halloween stories and Christmas stories but lamented the absence of decent stories about Thanksgiving—"I'm not talking about Pilgrims," she told Peck. "It was a hot day in November," Peck recalls, "and we walked into [a store] and it was full of Christmas tinsel and Santa Claus was already there. And I thought, what ever happened to Thanksgiving?" That became the working title of the book, which is about how people commercialize holidays and about a family that "has to look harder to find Thanksgiving."

12. Themes, Characters, and Style

"Few novelists perceive their audience as clearly as does Richard Peck," writes Janice Tovey in a scholarly analysis of Peck's young adult novels.

> His novels address the subjects and events which concern his audience and focus on problems to which they want answers. He writes to adolescents about themselves, their friends and peers and gets their attention by creating characters whom they recognize. He describes the families, the lifestyles, the towns, the societies and the cultures in which his audience lives. He mirrors adolescent fads in language and clothing. . . .
> By creating a community of discourse with his readers, Peck gains their trust and respect. He then confronts and challenges them to think about problems which they prefer to ignore, but which are important to them as individuals.[1]

Whether the topic is suicide or shopping malls, rape or romance, death or divorce, in 1914 or in 1988, one theme prevails in all of Richard Peck's novels: the importance of acting independently. In addition, as the previous examination of his novels reveals, Peck also focuses on social class differences, parental roles, ineffective schooling, friendships, male and female roles, the value of old people, and connections with the past.

In a 1976 interview Peck said: "In all of my novels, the main character takes a trip, a geographic trip. They all slip the bonds of peer group and family for an independent look at the world. Then they return, a bit more able to cope."[2] Although such a trip does not occur in some of his later novels—*Remembering the Good Times*, for example—it is certainly true of almost all others. His latest novel—*Those Summer Girls I Never Met*—contains the most extensive journey of all, most of the novel taking place on a cruise ship with stops in major European cities. Thus the physical journey enables the protagonist to make an intellectual and an emotional journey toward independence and understanding.

A small town in the Midwest, patterned after Peck's hometown in Illinois, provides the setting for three of his first four young adult novels, along with all four of the Blossom Culp books. By contrast, *Those Summer Girls*, his most recent novel, takes the reader to London, Copenhagen, and other European cities.

Three novels begin in New York but move the characters elsewhere for most of the story. Peck, in fact, avoids New York City as a setting for his young adult books (though not for his adult novels) because, he says, none of his readers live there. "The privately schooled youngster is really too pretentious for our books, and so are his teachers and librarians. And the public school student here is too illiterate to read. I get letters every day from readers, and have for nearly fifteen years. In all that time, I have had six letters from New York City."[3]

Peck's other novels are set in or around suburban areas. The suburban settings, based in part on his experience teaching in Northbrook, Illinois, provide Peck with ammunition for criticizing affluent parents for being too permissive, for not maintaining control over their children, and for being unable to communicate with them, problems that are shown most forcefully in *Remembering the Good Times*. In Peck's stories, it is often the less affluent parents who are more supportive of their children, as evidenced by Buck's father in *Remembering the Good Times* and by Verna's farm family in *Representing Super Doll*.

Older places not only have more character for Richard Peck, but they provide significant links to the past. One especially valuable aspect of the Blossom Culp novels is that they picture a place and time where life seems to be safer and more fun. At the same time, the emotions and basic problems of Blossom and Alexander are contemporary ones, like being accepted by the group, following the crowd blindly, and dealing with school boredom. Peck, making use of Blossom's ability to travel through time, whisks her from 1914 to the 1980s, where she makes comparisons with her "normal" life. She prefers 1914, certainly.

Probably the two most important elements that establish time and place in Richard Peck's novels are the teenagers' clothing and language. By carefully dressing his characters in contemporary fashions and having them use contemporary expressions, Peck lets readers know that he's informed, that he's in touch with what's important to them. For example, when Blossom is transported to the present age, she is confused by such brand names as Sears Toughskins and Adidas, while a group of Valley Girls at Jeremy's school speak a foreign language that includes "gross me out," "shanky," and "tubular." In *Close Enough to Touch*, readers find characters dressed in Jordache jeans, Nike and Puma sneakers, and other "preppie" clothing. And in *Remembering the Good Times*, all the Subs (for suburban kids) wear Izod shirts, L. L. Bean pants, and Docksider shoes, while Drew in *Those Summer Girls* checks his Swatch and wears a CB Windbreaker. In *Remembering the Good Times*, readers will find familiar expressions such as "gross," "macho," and "far out," while in *Those Summer Girls*, Drew is into "bagging babes."

The places that the characters frequent are also familiar landmarks to contemporary teenagers: Friendly's, Sizzler, and, naturally, McDonald's. (In *Those Summer Girls*, Drew and Steph, while in London, unexpectedly see "A couple of mini-golden arches . . . laminated onto a three-hundred-year-old wall.") The names of movie idols and music stars pop up occasionally, too—Emilio Estevez and Molly Ringwald, Culture Club and Cyndi Lauper—as well as the names of popular television programs—"Hill Street Blues" and "M*A*S*H."

The academic and social levels of Peck's narrators also provide significant reference points. Peck usually focuses on a teenager who is on the edge of the action, is not from an upper-middle-class suburban home, and may not be among the academically talented group in school. For example, in *Don't Look and It Won't Hurt*, Carol remarks, "Anybody's house looks good to me compared to my own." Verna, in *Representing Super Doll*, is not the center of attention in school; she's the farm girl bussed into the town high school. In *Remembering the Good Times*, Buck comes from a blue-collar family and is not an especially good student in school, providing a strong contrast to his wealthy friend Trav who is an outstanding student. And there is the unforgettable Blossom Culp, who lives on the other side of the (trolley) tracks and whose mother represents the lowest level of Bluff City society. All of these characters, however, are especially good observers, even if, like Buck in *Remembering the Good Times* or Chelsea in *Princess Ashley*, they cannot instantly figure out what's going on. These characters are thus easier for the "average" student to identify with.

In their analysis of the best books written for young adults prior to 1980, Donelson and Nilsen point out that although nearly half the young adult novels written by women have a male narrator or lead character, Richard Peck is one of the few male writers who write from the perspective of female characters.[4] In fact, more than half of Peck's novels have a female narrator or are from a female's point of view.

With the exception of Chelsea in *Princess Ashley*, the female protagonists in Peck's young adult novels tend to be intellectually adept, insightful, and very independent. Kate in *Remembering the Good Times* and Margaret in *Close Enough to Touch*, are prime examples. They are both candid, cool, and self-assured, far more in tune with the world and themselves than the male lead characters in those novels. And Blossom Culp's spunk and resilience—not to mention her Second Sight—put her in a class by herself.

The male protagonists, on the other hand, are not stereotypical macho heroes. In fact, Jim in *Father Figure*, Matt in *Close Enough to Touch*, and Buck in *Remembering the Good Times* are some of the most sensitive male characters in all of young adult literature. They tend to be average guys instead of leaders, though Blossom Culp's cohort Alexander Armsworth performs heroic deeds, usually against his own better judgment.

Relationships between males and females in Peck's young adult novels are usually platonic, never sexual—with, of course, the exception of *Are You in the House Alone?*, where Gail has had sex with her boyfriend and is later raped by another boy, and the pregnancy that occurs with the narrator's older sister in *Don't Look and It Won't Hurt*. In *Through a Brief Darkness*, Karen is attracted to Jay who helps rescue her; in *Super Doll*, Verna is squired around New York City by a young man; and in *Secrets of the Shopping Mall*, Teresa and Barnie spend most of their days and nights together. But there is no more than hand-holding and a very chaste exchange of kisses in those stories. Although Matt in *Close Enough to Touch* was on the verge of having a sexual relationship with Dory, she died before they got that far, and at the end of the novel he and Margaret are just beginning to become physically close. Drew in *Those Summer Girls* has lustful thoughts about women, but he is somewhat inept, as well as immature, in his dealings with the female dancers on the cruise ship and so gets little more than sisterly hugs and kisses along with an eyeful of gorgeous flesh from them. In short, friendships are more important than sexual relationships in Richard Peck's young adult novels.

That is not the case in his adult novels, as one might predict. There is a fair amount of sexual activity in those three novels, though none of it very explicit. The women in those novels are stronger and more admirable than the men, though Amanda is a despicable manipulator. Interestingly, Richard Peck has not yet written an adult novel with a male protagonist. "I keep starting it," he reports. "I've got this guy driving down the Hutchinson River Parkway [which leads into and out of New York City] in the middle of his life and I get to the end of the chapter and I say, oh god, who's going to want to read this? Who's going to want to see how a man in middle life not only suffers but can't show it?" And that's as far as he's gone.

As the discussion of individual novels showed earlier, parents play significant roles in Richard Peck's young adult books. Some parents are supportive—like Matt's father in *Close Enough to Touch*, Buck's father in *Remembering the Good Times*, and Verna's parents, especially her mother, in *Representing Super Doll*. Other parents are too permissive, out of touch with their children, or just never around— like the absent father and the harried mother in *Don't Look*, Blossom

Culp's bizarre gypsy mother, and Trav's wealthy parents in *Remembering the Good Times*. Some other parents are too domineering—like Darlene's mother in *Super Doll* and Dory's socialite mother in *Close Enough to Touch*. A few parents try to help but struggle as much as their children do—like Jim and Byron's father in *Father Figure* and Chelsea's mother in *Princess Ashley*.

A preponderance of the parents of the main characters in Richard Peck's novels are divorced or otherwise living without a partner. In only five of Peck's fifteen young adult novels does the main character live with both biological parents, and in most of those novels the parents of other characters are divorced. In the most extreme cases, neither lead character in *Secrets of the Shopping Mall*, has biological parents and in *Those Summer Girls*, Drew's grandfather has never been aware that he even sired a daughter.

Some of Peck's fathers—Matt's and Buck's in particular—are unusually understanding, sharing their feelings and helping their respective sons deal with their own emotions. Such male roles are noticeably lacking in most other young adult fiction and so are doubly welcome in Peck's novels, especially since they are in such contrast to Gail's ineffectual father in *Are You in the House Alone?* and Chelsea's psychologically damaged father in *Princess Ashley*.

Two mother figures—though neither of them is a biological mother—are worth singling out for their supportive roles. Marietta, Mr. Atwater's girlfriend in *Father Figure*, is not only important for the self-concept she projects, but, in her own way, she also mothers both Jim and his younger brother, deflecting Jim's Oedipal advances and helping him deal with his relationship with his previously estranged father. And in *Close Enough to Touch*, Beth Moran is one of the most supportive stepmothers in young adult literature. In contrast to Buck's parents, Tovey notes, "Beth Moran works to give love and support to her stepson without forcing herself into the role of mother."[5]

An old person is a prominent figure in nine of Peck's young adult novels, all but Jim Atwater's grandmother in *Father Figure* having a positive influence. All are women, except for the nosy, crotchety, free-spirited Great Uncle Miles in the *The Ghost Belonged to Me*. Some are the main character's grandmother; some are someone else's grandmother; some are teachers; others are just an old resident of the town with whom the main characters interact. All of them are spunky, eccentric, and wise, providing a nostalgic link to the past when life seemed simpler and more in control. Top honors in this category go to the balding, gold-toothed, wheelchair-bound Polly Prior, Kate's great-grandmother in *Remembering the Good Times*, and to Drew and Stephanie's grandmother, Connie Carlson, the terminally ill jazz singer from the forties. They provide positive images of significant old people for contemporary readers who often have little or no contact with their own grandparents.

There is at least one teacher in every one of Richard Peck's novels (except for *Those Summer Girls I Never Met*, because that takes place entirely during the summer). The images that these teachers project as a group are not positive, though there are some good teachers— Madam Malevich, for one—among the group. The majority of them, understandably, are English teachers, though a few are teachers of social studies, physical education, and—Peck's least favorite— Contemporary Social Issues. Educators who choose to analyze the teaching techniques of ex-teacher Peck's fictional faculty will find a variety of approaches, most of them unproductive.

The most evident technique used by Mrs. DeFalco to teach social studies in an inter-city junior high school in *Secrets of the Shopping Mall*, for example, is to scream for quiet. Miss Winkler's main preoccupation in *The Ghost Belonged to Me* is checking each student for clean hands and a clean handkerchief (of course, that was in 1913). In 1980, Mrs. Tolliver, teaching British Literature in *Close Enough to Touch*, uses photocopied worksheets continually, though she does help Matt reach some understanding of a poem by Gerard Manley Hopkins when he approaches her for independent help after class. The least prepared teacher is Ms. Sherrie Slater in *Remembering the Good Times*, a first-year teacher who cannot control her junior high school students and so is transferred to the high school where she does no better. Trav sums up the good students' view of their education in Ms. Slater's class when he complains: "I'm coasting. We're all coasting. This is recess." Probably the worst educator of all is the guidance counselor, Miss Venable, in *Are You in the House Alone?*, who is completely unable to help Gail or deal with the threatening notes Gail finds in her locker.

Other school administrators are no better. In *Father Figure*, the headmaster from Byron's school, Mr. Brewster Stewart, is concerned more about his school's reputation than about the condition of one of his students who has been mugged on the way home from school. In *Remembering the Good Times*, no administrator is visible when Skeeter explodes. When one of the school's best students commits suicide, the school's administration calls a community meeting to discuss the problem but takes no responsibility for helping students cope with what they see as "'a problem essentially rooted in home and family.'" And in *Princess Ashley*, when a disturbed student physically attacks Mrs. Olinger, the school's administration does nothing about it; no one from the school even visits Mrs. Olinger in the hospital, only the school secretary phones to see how she is.

The most positive teachers in Peck's novels are demanding but fair and concerned. Miss Klimer in *Dreamland Lake*, "believed strongly in Written Expression." Miss Castle, in *Super Doll*, is "a spacey and sweetly strange spinster" who Verna characterizes as "a lady of the old school." Miss Augusta Fairweather in *Blossom Culp and the Sleep of Death*, a former suffragette, puts her students through their paces in studying Egypt. The most admirable teacher is Mr. Mallory, an exchange teacher from Great Britain, in *Princess Ashley*. He sets high standards in his creative writing class, but he is also a caring person. Chelsea in retrospect says, "Mr. Mallory had been our hardest teacher and we never knew it."

Several structural qualities are worth noting in Peck's novels. In almost all of his stories, a key crisis or turning point occurs in nearly the exact middle of the novel. The middle chapter of *Through a Brief Darkness*, for example, is the point at which Karen vows to "get to the bottom of it all" and then discovers for certain that she is a prisoner. In the exact middle of *Father Figure*, Jim and Byron arrive in Florida to begin a new life with their father. Just before the middle page of *Princess Ashley*, Chelsea's mother is attacked by Gloria, thus revealing the school connection between Mrs. Olinger and Chelsea. The middle of *Remembering the Good Times* finds Kate, Trav, and Buck at the start of their freshman year, where only a few pages later, Trav yells at Ms. Slater for not teaching them anything and she reveals that she is being harassed by Skeeter.

That midpoint crisis is often tied in with Peck's method of revealing tantalizing fragments of information that create mystery and keep readers turning pages to find out what will happen. In *Dreamland Lake*, for example, the reader learns only bits and pieces about pitiable Elvan Helligrew and his preoccupation with Nazi memorabilia and what that has to do with the dead man in the amusement park. Even though Brian is telling the story two years later, he keeps readers in suspense until the sudden tragic ending. Similarly, in *Princess Ashley*, the school connection between Chelsea and her mother is kept from readers until the midpoint in the novel in the same way that Chelsea wanted it to be kept from her peers in school. And in *Those Summer Girls*, Drew (and the reader) doesn't learn until nearly the end of the cruise—and the end of the novel—why his grandmother has suddenly wanted to spend time with him and his sister after years of not seeing them.

Peck frequently uses foreshadowing to help the reader anticipate future events as well as to encourage reading on. That's especially easy in the Blossom Culp novels, of course, because Blossom or her mother can see into the future and make cryptic predictions. The reader is compelled to read on to see what it means when Blossom is told, for instance, that she will take two trips over water, one of them in the past that has been "'interrupted . . . by death.'" In other novels, the narrator sometimes gives a hint of future complications. In *Dreamland Lake*, for example, after Brian and Flip have returned Elvan's German sword to him, Brian says, "It was like buying him off. I wish we had." In *Are You in the House Alone?*, Gail, finding her mother sitting alone in a darkened house with a drink in her hand, says, "Neither the darkness nor the drink seemed odd at the time." Carol, in *Don't Look*, says, "I thought things couldn't look worse. I was wrong." Peck employs this technique most extensively in his first adult novel, *Amanda/Miranda*. For example, Miranda says at one point, "we had seemed to skirt a small lovers' quarrel. I had no premonition of a greater crisis ahead."

In addition, most of Peck's novels end without a solution. That is not to suggest that the reader is left hanging, only that there are no pat answers to some of the problems. For example, at the end of *Don't Look and It Won't Hurt*, Carol returns home from visiting her pregnant sister in Chicago, still unsure if Ellen will be coming back to join the family. At the end of *Father Figure*, Jim has come to terms with leaving his brother Byron with his father while he himself returns to New York City. But that means he still has to live for another year with his cold and incommunicative grandmother. At the end of *Remembering the Good Times*, Buck and Kate are together and life goes on, but Trav is dead and there is nothing they can do about it. And Gail, in *Are You in the House Alone?*, knows her rapist remains unpunished, even though she has done one small thing to get back at him. The endings, while not necessarily happy, are credible and appropriate.

Another distinctive mark of Richard Peck's style is his ability to include comedy and wit even in novels about the most serious subjects. His most recent novel, *Those Summer Girls I Never Met*, deals in part with the fatal illness of the teenagers' grandmother. Yet the novel is one of Peck's most humorous. The humor, of course, is not about death, but the comic incidents keep the novel from becoming bleak.

Humor in Peck's books is evidenced in events themselves—the commotion caused by Blossom's accidentally setting fire to Old Man Leverette's outhouse, for example—as well as in characters and language. The character of Daisy-Rae in *The Dreadful Future of Blossom Culp*, for example, is worth a laugh nearly every time she appears. Most of the time she is found hiding in one of the stalls of the girls' room at school, determined never to enter a classroom. Her brother Roderick, a "medium simple," "apathetic little gnome" of a kid, never speaks a word throughout the entire novel, though he does drool at appropriate times. Miss Dabney, in *Ghosts I have Been*, is certainly eccentric, though not as peculiar as the deranged ghost of a kitchen maid who trashes her kitchen on a daily basis until Blossom calms her down. When Drew and Steph walk the streets of London in *Those Summer Girls*, one of the sights they see is a group of punkers. Half of the hair of one of them, "day-glo orange, is standing up like an enraged porcupine." Another one's hair is in dreadlocks, "no two the same color, like the rainbow in an oil slick." A third is wearing "an evening gown, orange, under a combat jacket." Compared to Steph's "three puny little gold hoops" in one ear, the punkers "have this much hardware in their noses," Drew notes.

Peck, of course, includes the appropriate language to accompany any such scene, whether it's spoken by punkers, Valley Girls, or preppies. One of Blossom's more characteristic uses of language —in addition to her less-than-standard English (e.g., "Miss Dabney and me were loud in our praise")—is clichés. Her narration abounds with such chestnuts as "always darkest before the dawn," "keep my sunny side up," "took the bull by the horns," and "No use cryin' over spilt milk."

There are, intentionally, no vulgarities in Peck's novels. "I am very careful of the language—much more careful than I want to be," Peck says. "I work pretty hard to keep the language cleaner in my books than the language of my readers. . . . I don't want my books to be kept out of the hands of readers for the wrong reasons."

Peck's concern with language is also evident in the abundance of word play in his novels, especially in the Blossom Culp books. For example, Alexander says in *The Ghost Belonged to Me*, "I knew she hadn't eaten anything since Friday noon in order to get into her coming out dress." In *Blossom Culp and the Sleep of Death*, while studying Egyptian history, Alexander says about the Rosetta stone: "That lump of rock is a millstone around my neck."

It is evident that Richard Peck enjoys himself as he writes. "I like the uses of humor in writing," he says. "I like satire. I like word play. I like whole comic scenes. I like humor to serious intent." He even has fun with characters' names. There's Bertha Small, the huge security guard in the department store in *Secrets of the Shopping Mall*. In *Are You in the House Alone?*, there is the inept guidance counselor, Miss Venable, who is not venerable but is rather vulnerable instead. Darlene is the darling beauty queen in *Super Doll*. And if Fairweather isn't an appropriate enough name for a supportive teacher (in *Sleep of Death*), then Mallory is as good a name as you'll find for a British English teacher (in *Princess Ashley*). Speaking of Ashley herself, with a last name of Packard, how can she (ironically) be anything else but classy?

One final characteristic of Peck's use of language as a stylistic benchmark is his employment of aphorisms. Although they are sometimes a bit more erudite than the maturity of the teenager speaking them would warrant, they allow Peck to make comments on people, school, society—all his favorite targets—throughout his novels. For example, in *Remembering the Good Times*, Buck says "It's funny how much you want to work before you're old enough to hold a job." Or later he remarks, "At that age, when there's something you can't explain, you walk away from it." In *Princess Ashley*, Chelsea says, "At our age, who wants a mother?" and "[I]n tenth grade you like rumors better than the truth anyway."

Richard Peck continues to teach in every novel he writes, although he says, "I don't really believe my books are going to change people's lives." But some books obviously do hit home:

> I get letters from young people who say, "I'm the character in your book." or "It happens here." I want that to happen, because I want young people to think that what's in a book is just as real and important as what is in their lives and a whole lot more important than television. . . . But I can't preach it; I've got to write something entertaining about it.[6]

What will the next book be about? Peck calls it "a funny fantasy" in the Blossom Culp mold, though with "a new cast of characters and a different setting." The working title is *Voices after Midnight*. It will undoubtedly be entertaining—and it will undoubtedly sneak in a lesson with the fun.

Appendix A: Honors and Prizes

Amanda/Miranda

Literary Guild Selection
Reader's Digest Condensed Book

Are You in the House Alone?

Best Books for Young Adults, 1976, American Library Association
Best of the Best Books 1970–82, Young Adult Services Division, American
  Library Association
Best Books of the Year, 1976, *School Library Journal*
Edgar Allan Poe Mystery Award, 1977
Books for Young Adults Poll, 1977, University of Iowa
Nominated for Colorado Blue Spruce Young Adult Book Award, 1986

Blossom Culp and the Sleep of Death

American Library Association Notable Books for Children, 1986

Close Enough to Touch

Best Books for Young Adults, 1981, American Library Association
Nominated for Colorado Blue Spruce Young Adult Book Award, 1987

Dreamland Lake

Edgar Allan Poe Special Mystery Award, 1973

Father Figure

Best Books for Young Adults, 1978, American Library Association
Best of the Best Books 1970–82, Young Adult Services Division, American
    Library Association
Nominated for Colorado Blue Spruce Young Adult Book Award, 1985

The Ghost Belonged to Me

American Library Association Notable Books for Children, 1975
Friends of American Writers Award, 1976

Ghosts I Have Been

Best Books for Young Adults, 1977, American Library Association
Best of the Best Books 1970–82, Young Adult Services Division, American
    Library Association
Best Books of the Year, 1977, *School Library Journal*
New York Times Outstanding Books of the Year, 1977
Nominated for 1980 Michigan Young Readers Award

Princess Ashley

American Library Association Notable Books for Children, 1987
Best Books for Young Adults, 1987, American Library Association
Best Books of the Year, 1987, *School Library Journal*
Nominated for Colorado Blue Spruce Young Adult Book Award, 1988

Remembering the Good Times

Best Books for Young Adults, 1985, American Library Association
Best Books of the Year, 1985, *School Library Journal*
Books for Young Adults Poll, 1986, University of Iowa
Nominated for Dorothy Canfield Fisher Children's Book Award

Representing Superdoll

Best Books for Young Adults, 1974, American Library Association
Books for Young Adults Poll, 1975, University of Iowa

This Family of Women

Books for Young Adults Poll, 1984, University of Iowa
Doubleday Book Club Alternate
Literary Guild Alternate

General Awards

Illinois Writer of the Year (chosen by the Illinois Association of Teachers of
  English), 1977
National Council for the Advancement of Education Writing Award, 1971

Appendix B: Film Adaptations

The Ghost Belonged to Me

Richard Peck's first novel in the Blossom Culp series was filmed by Walt Disney Productions as a television movie and appeared in 1977 on what is now called the "Wonderful World of Disney" under the title *Child of Glass*. It stars Barbara Barrie and Biff McGuire.

Peck is not pleased with the film. He had no access to the filmscript and little contact with the people who made the movie. (The same was true for the films of his other novels.) About specifics, Peck says:

> They promised to keep the name of the book—and they changed it within two weeks of airing. They turned the great-uncle in my novel, who is a portrait of my own great-uncle, Uncle Miles—who is the kind of old man the young boy [Alexander] would like to be one day—they turned him into an alcoholic murderer. And they set the novel in the present [instead of the original 1913], perhaps to save money on period sets and costumes.

It usually reappears each year on television around Halloween, Peck says with a sigh.

[This ninety-four-minute film is available from Walt Disney Films.]

Are You in the House Alone?

Peck's sixth novel for young adults was adapted for a two-hour television movie by CBS-TV and had its first run during prime time in 1978. Capitalizing on the topical rape issue, the film begins with Gail being taken to the hospital after the rape and then flashes back to the start of Gail's story. She says, "I can't tell anybody. They won't believe me." And so the film shows how her attacker, the son of the wealthiest family in town, pursued her and what the aftermath was.

Richard Peck was pleased with the casting of this film, which stars Kathleen Beller as Gail, Dennis Quaid as the rapist, and Blythe Danner as Gail's mother. Probably for the sake of convenience, the setting was changed from suburban Connecticut to Marin County, California, a change that reflected some of the social differences though not the small town attitudes that are an important basis of the novel. Other changes in Judith Parker's script transform the mother for whom Gail babysits into a lawyer, allow Gail's boyfriend to know who the attacker is, and reshape the unsympathetic male police chief into a slightly less offensive female officer. The change that most disturbs Richard Peck, however, is the ending of the film: Gail sets a trap for Phil that leads to his being tried and convicted of the lesser charge of assault. Peck's purpose in writing the book was to show that there is no justice in our society when it comes to a case like Gail's and to raise the question of what then can the victim do about it. As Peck explains it: "How are you going to arrange your life now that you've found out that life is not a party, that the crooks aren't caught? But in the film the crook is caught! Which invalidates the book as far as I'm concerned."

Leonard Maltin calls the film an "unsatisfactory adaptation" of Peck's novel,[1] and Steven Scheuer says, "This clanky TV movie thriller was not worthy of the neat suspense novel on which it was based."[2] But it could have been worse, and it does provide some insight into the feelings of a courageous teenager who has little support from friends, parents, and society.

[The ninety-six-minute video of this film, made by Stonehenge Productions, is available from Worldvision Home Video, Inc.]

Father Figure

Maltin calls this made-for-television movie an "affecting drama,"[3] and it is the best of the three dramatizations of Peck's novels. Although the William Hanley screenplay, which first aired on CBS-TV in October 1980, holds together quite well, the story's perspective is shifted from the seventeen-year-old son, played by Timothy Hutton, to the middle-aged father, played by Hal Linden. Janet Seigel, in "From Page to Screen: Where the Author Fits In," explains that film producers and directors, although they like the stories that young adult novels contain, "rarely let the books speak for themselves." In almost every case, Seigel maintains, the role of the adult in the story is "magnified in order to attract an established adult star, ensuring adequate financing for production."[4] That is true of the mother's role that Blythe Danner played in *Are You in the House Alone?*, and it is especially true of Hal Linden's role in *Father Figure*.

In the novel, the father is "a low-key figure," Peck says, a drop-out from life who is "quite in love with a young woman but he has no way to get her—

not as a wife, not as a mistress." But in the scene in the film where the father is introduced, he's lying in bed with his mistress who is pleading with him to marry her. Some of the other differences between the film and the book are significant, others are not. But Richard Peck is pleased that the film at least ends in the same way his novel does. "That's an achievement," he says. "And it's the right ending."

[The video of this ninety-five-minute film, made by Time-Life Productions, is available from Lightning Video International.]

Other Novels

In 1975 Peck announced that Walt Disney Productions had purchased the rights to *Through a Brief Darkness* and was about to start filming it with the then popular Linda Blair in the starring role.[5] But the film was never made. And at the 1981 ALA annual conference in San Francisco, Peck announced that *Close Enough to Touch* was soon to be filmed for television by MGM.[6] That was followed by an article in the *Boston Herald American* in 1982 stating that *Close Enough to Touch* had been "filmed for television."[7] But no film was ever made of that novel. Richard Peck indicates that while most of his novels have been optioned for television films, only the three noted above have yet been made.

Notes and References

Chapter 1

1. "Best of the Best Books 1970–82," *Booklist*, 15 October 1983, 351–54.

2. Donald R. Gallo, "Who Are the Most Important YA Authors?" *The ALAN Review*, Spring 1989, 18–20.

3. All quotations of Richard Peck's statements throughout this book that are not attributed to a specific published source come from my correspondence with him or my personal interviews with him that took place in his New York City apartment in early June and late December 1987, unless otherwise noted.

4. Richard Peck, in Viking Press publicity brochure, n.d.

5. Richard Peck, speech presented at the Children's Book Council / American Booksellers Association meeting, New Orleans, 24 May 1986; also printed as "Young Adult Books" in *Horn Book*, September–October 1986, 619.

6. Richard Peck, speech presented at the Children's Literature Festival, University of Southern Mississippi, Hattiesburg, 19 March 1981.

7. Richard Peck, quoted by Lou Willett Stanek in "Just Listening: Interviews with Six Adolescent Novelists: Patricia McKillip, Robert Cormier, Norma Klein, Richard Peck, S. E. Hinton, Judy Blume," *Arizona English Bulletin*, April 1976, 32.

8. Peck, Children's Literature Festival, University of Southern Mississippi.

9. Ibid.

10. Marilou Sorenson, *Deseret News*, 29 January 1984.

11. *Kirkus*, 1 May 1987, 724.

12. Mary K. Chelton, *Voice of Youth Advocates*, October 1981, 36.

13. *Publishers Weekly*, 2 October 1981, 111.

14. Cynthia K. Leibold, *School Library Journal*, April 1985, 9.

15. Denise A. Anton, *School Library Journal*, August 1987, 97.

16. Evie Wilson, *Voice of Youth Advocates*, June 1987, 82.

17. Richard Peck, "A Writer from Illinois," *Illinois Libraries*, June 1986, 392.

18. Ibid., 393.

19. Richard Peck, *Something about the Author Autobiography Series*, vol. 2, ed. Adele Sarkissian (Detroit: Gale Research, 1985), 178.

20. Ibid., 177.

21. Ibid., 178.

22. Peck, "A Writer from Illinois," 393.

23. Richard Peck, "The Invention of Adolescence and Other Thoughts on Youth," *Top of the News*, Winter 1983, 182.

24. Peck, "A Writer from Illinois," 393.

25. Peck, *Something about the Author Autobiography Series*, vol. 2:178.

26. Peck, "The Invention of Adolescence," 183.

27. Ibid.

28. Richard Peck in *Speaking for Ourselves*, ed. Donald R. Gallo, in preparation.

29. Peck, "A Writer from Illinois," 394.

30. Ibid.

31. Peck, *Something about the Author Autobiography Series*, vol. 2:180.

32. Ibid., 181.

33. Richard Peck, quoted by Jean W. Ross in *Contemporary Authors*, New Revision Series, vol. 19, ed. Linda Metzger (Detroit: Gale Research, 1987), 368.

34. Peck, *Something about the Author Autobiography Series*, vol. 2:181.

35. Ibid.

36. Ibid., 182.

37. Ibid.

38. Peck, Viking Press publicity brochure.

39. Peck, *Something about the Author Autobiography Series*, vol. 2:183.

40. Peck, Viking Press publicity brochure.

41. Richard Peck, "Coming Full Circle: From Lesson Plans to Young Adult Novels," *Horn Book*, April 1985, 209.

42. Peck, *Something about the Author Autobiography Series*, vol. 2:183.

43. Peck, "Coming Full Circle," 210.

44. Ibid., 211.

45. Nancy Gallt, telephone interview, 22 July 1988.

46. Peck, "Coming Full Circle," 212.

47. Ibid., 213.

48. Richard Peck, quoted in *Contemporary Authors*, 85–88, ed. Frances Carol Locher (Detroit: Gale Research, 1980), 459.

49. Peck, Viking Press publicity brochure.

50. Ibid.

51. Curt Schleler, "Peck Is Author Whose Dreams Came True," *Grand Rapids Press*, 25 July 1982.

52. "A Conversation with Richard Peck," Dell Publishing Company publicity brochure, n.d.

53. Schleler, "Dreams Came True."

54. Dell Publishing Company publicity brochure, November 1988, 6.

Chapter 2

1. Peck, Children's Literature Festival, University of Southern Mississippi.

2. Richard Peck, interview at Montclair (New Jersey) Public Library, 9 December 1987.

3. Peck, *Something about the Author Autobiography Series*, vol. 2:184.

4. Peck, quoted by Jean W. Ross, *Contemporary Authors*, New revision Series, vol. 19, 367.

5. Peck, "Coming Full Circle," 214.

6. Peck, interview, Montclair (New Jersey) Public Library.

7. Ibid.

8. Ibid.

9. Ibid.

10. Peck, quoted by Jean W. Ross, *Contemporary Authors*, New Revision Series, vol. 19, 369.

11. Ibid.

12. Richard Peck, workshop at Montclair (New Jersey) Public Library, 9 December 1987.

13. Peck, quoted by Jean W. Ross, *Contemporary Authors*, New Revision Series, vol. 19, 370.

14. Peck, "The Invention of Adolescence," 186.

15. Ibid.

16. Ibid., 187.

Chapter 3

1. Peck, interview at Montclair (New Jersey) Public Library.

2. Peck, Children's Literature Festival, University of Southern Mississippi.

3. Randi Sulkin, "Richard Peck: Writing Is Communication," *Ketchikan Daily News*, 3–9 March 1984, 2.

4. Patrice Smith, "Author Aims at Teen-Age Ideals," *Evansville Courier*, n.d.

5. Peck, workshop at Montclair (New Jersey) Public Library, 9 December 1987.

6. "Tips That Get Kids Reading," *Ketchikan Daily News*, 3-9 March 1984, 3.

7. Richard Peck, "Some Thoughts on Adolescent Lit.," *News from ALAN*, September-October 1975, 4.

8. Peck, interview at Montclair (New Jersey) Public Library.

9. Richard Peck, "Ten Questions to Ask about a Novel," *ALAN Newsletter*, Spring 1978, 1.

10. Peck, "The Invention of Adolescence," 188.

11. Ibid., 188-189.

12. Ibid., 189.

13. Ibid., 190.

14. Richard Peck, "Care and Feeding of the Visiting Author," *Top of the News*, Spring 1982, 251-55.

15. Richard Peck, "A Teenager's Prayer," in "Young Adult Books," *Horn Book*, September-October 1968, 621.

16. Richard Peck, "The Fervent Prayer of a Teenager's Parent," *The ALAN Review*, Winter 1987, 51.

17. Richard Peck, "A Teacher's Prayer," *News from Dell Books*, n.d.

Chapter 4

1. Richard Peck, *Leap into Reality: Essays for Now* (New York: Dell, 1973), 10.

2. Richard Peck, "It's a World Away and Yet So Close," *New York Times*, 8 October 1972, 4.

3. Richard Peck, "St. Charles Is the Last Trolley Left," *New York Times*, 28 January 1973, 3, 17.

4. Richard Peck, "Consciousness-Raising," *American Libraries*, February 1974, 75.

5. Richard Peck, "Delivering the Goods," *American Libraries*, October 1974, 492.

6. Richard Peck, "We Can Save Our Schools," *Parents' Magazine and Better Family Living*, September 1971, 51.

7. Ibid.

8. Richard Peck, "Can Students Evaluate Their Education?" *PTA Magazine*, February 1971, 4.

9. Peck, "We Can Save Our Schools," 100.

10. Ibid., 99.

11. Richard Peck, "People of the World: A Look at Today's Young Adults and Their Needs," *School Library Media Quarterly*, Fall 1981, 17.

12. Ibid., 18.

13. Ibid., 19.

14. Richard Peck, "Growing Up Suburban: 'We Don't Use Slang, We're Gifted,'" in "In the YA Corner," *School Library Journal*, October 1985, 119.

15. Peck, "People of the World," 20.

16. Peck, "Growing Up Suburban," 119.

17. Richard Peck, "In the Country of Teenage Fiction," *American Libraries*, April 1973, 204–07.

18. Peck, "The Invention of Adolescence," 182–90.

19. Richard Peck, "YA Books in the Decade of the Vanishing Adult," *Dell Carousel*, Fall–Winter 1985–86, 1–2.

20. Peck, "Some Thoughts on Adolescent Literature," 5–6.

21. Peck, "Ten Questions to Ask about a Novel," 1, 7.

22. Peck, "Care and Feeding of the Visiting Author," 251–55.

23. Richard Peck, "The Genteel Unshelving of a Book," *School Library Journal*, May 1986, 37–39.

Chapter 5

1. Richard Peck, in "Phoenix Nest," ed. Martin Levin, *Saturday Review*, 4 September 1971, 6.

2. Richard Peck, in "Phoenix Nest," ed. Martin Levin, *Saturday Review*, 21 June 1969, 6.

3. Peck, *Mindscapes*, 8.

4. Richard Peck, in *Sports Poems*, ed. R. R. Knudson and P. K. Ebert (New York: Dell, 1971), 142.

5. Richard Peck, *Sounds and Silences: Poetry for Now* (New York: Dell, 1970), 9.

6. Richard Peck, *Chicago Tribune Magazine*, 17 September 1972.

7. *Christian Science Monitor*, 27 January 1971.

8. *Saturday Review*, 19 September 1970, 35.

9. John W. Conner, *English Journal*, September 1971, 830.

10. Walter Clemons, *New York Times Book Review*, 27 June 1971, 8.

11. *Kirkus Reviews*, 1 March 1971, 244.

12. *Booklist*, 15 July 1971, 952.

13. Margaret A. Dorsey, *Library Journal*, 15 June 1971, 2140.

14. *Booklist*, 1 December 1976, 532.

15. Sarajean Marks, *School Library Journal*, May 1977, 71.

16. Marilou Sorensen, *Deseret News*, Fall 1981.

17. Richard Peck, *Pictures That Storm Inside My Head: Poems for the Inner You* (New York: Avon, 1976), 23.

18. Ibid., 173.

19. Marks, 71.

Chapter 6

1. Richard Peck, dust jacket for *Princess Ashley*, Delacorte Press, 1987.
2. Peggy Sullivan, *Library Journal*, 15 December 1972, 4080.
3. *Booklist*, 15 February 1973, 574.
4. *Kirkus Reviews*, 15 August 1972, 949.
5. *Publishers Weekly*, 25 September 1972, 60.
6. Sheila Schwartz, *Teaching Adolescent Literature: A Humanistic Approach* (Rochelle Park, N.J.: Hayden Book Company, 1979), 201–02.
7. Ibid., 202.
8. Alice H. Yucht, *School Library Journal*, 15 November 1973, 53.
9. *Kirkus Reviews*, 15 June 1973, 648.
10. *New York Times Book Review*, 13 January 1974, 10.
11. *Publishers Weekly*, 6 August 1973, 65.
12. *Kirkus Reviews*, 648.
13. *Booklist*, 15 November 1973, 342.
14. Margery Fisher, "Fashion in Adventure," *Growing Point*, April 1976, 2844–48 in *Contemporary Literary Criticism*, vol. 21, ed. Sharon R. Gunton (Detroit: Gale Research Company, 1982), 298.
15. Peggy Sullivan, *School Library Journal*, February 1974, 72.
16. *Kirkus Reviews*, 1 December 1973, 1314.
17. *Booklist*, 1 October 1974, 159.
18. *Publishers Weekly*, 9 September 1974, 68.
19. Zena Sutherland, *Bulletin of the Center for Children's Books*, November 1974, 51.
20. Jean Alexander, *The Washington Post Book World*, 10 November 1974, 8.
21. Richard Peck, interviewed by Paul Janeczko, *From Writers to Students: The Pleasures and Pains of Writing*, ed. M. Jerry Weiss (Newark, Del.: International Reading Association, 1979), 80.

Chapter 7

1. Peck, speech at Children's Literature Festival, University of Southern Mississippi.
2. Paul Janeczko, "An Interview with Richard Peck," *English Journal*, February 1976, 97.
3. Richard Peck, "An Exclusive Interview with Blossom Culp," Dell Publishing Company publicity brochure, 1987.
4. Ibid.
5. Ibid.
6. Peck, *Something about the Author Autobiography Series*, 178.

7. Alleen P. Nilsen and Kenneth L. Donelson, *Literature for Today's Young Adults*, 2nd ed. (Glenview, Ill.: Scott, Foresman and Company, 1985), 153.

8. Ibid., 153–54.

9. Barbara Elleman, "50 Books Too Good to Be Missed," *Learning*, April–May 1985, 28.

10. *Booklist*, 1 July 1975, 1129.

11. Judith Atwater, *School Library Journal*, September 1975, 109.

12. *The Junior Bookshelf*, June 1977, 183.

13. Joan Goldman Levine, *New York Times*, 27 July 1975, 8.

14. Bruce Clements, *Psychology Today*, September 1975, 75.

15. Hillary Crew, "Blossom Culp and Her Ilk: The Independent Female in Richard Peck's YA Fiction," *Top of the News*, Spring 1987, 300.

16. Peck, workshop at Montclair (New Jersey) Public Library.

17. Richard Peck, "A Personal Letter from: Blossom Culp to: Whom It May Concern," Dell Publishing Company publicity brochure, n.d.

18. Tony Manna, *The ALAN Review*, Fall 1979.

19. Linda Silver, *School Library Journal*, November 1977, 61.

20. Ethel L. Heins, *Horn Book*, February 1978, 56.

21. Jane B. Jackson, *Kliatt Young Adult Paperback Book Guide*, Fall 1979, 12.

22. Peck, "A Personal Letter from Blossom Culp."

23. Patricia Lee Gauch, *New York Times Book Review*, 18 December 1983, 21.

24. *Ocala Star Banner*, 25 December 1984.

25. Ethel L. Heins, *Horn Book*, February 1984, 64.

26. Anne Eliot Crompton, *Parents' Choice*, Spring–Summer 1984, 5.

27. Patty Campbell, *Wilson Library Bulletin*, March 1986, 51.

28. Michael Cart, *School Library Journal*, May 1986, 108.

29. *Publishers Weekly*, 21 March 1986.

Chapter 8

1. Richard Peck, "Richard Peck Discusses Adolescent Rape," Dell Publishing Company publicity release, n.d.

2. Peck, interviewed by Paul Janeczko in *From Writers to Students*, 81.

3. Richard Peck, "Rape and the Teenage Victim," *Top of the News*, Winter 1978, 175–76.

4. Ibid., 175.

5. Janet Leonberger, *Young Adult Cooperative Book Review Group of Massachusetts*, February 1977, 89.

6. Zena Sutherland, *Bulletin for the Center for Children's Books*, March 1977, 112.

7. Paul Heins, *Horn Book*, February 1977, 60.

8. J. W. Levy, *Journal of Reading*, April 1978, 655.

9. Alix Nelson, *New York Times Book Review*, 14 November 1976, 29.

10. G. Robert Carlsen, Connie Bennett, and Ann Harker, "1977 Books for Young Adults Poll," *English Journal*, January 1978, 91–92.

11. *Publishers Weekly*, 17 July 1978, 168.

12. James T. Henke, "The Death of the Mother, the Rebirth of the Son: *Millie's Boy* and *Father Figure*," *Children's Literature in Education*, Spring 1983, 21–34.

13. Peck, quoted by Jean W. Ross, *Contemporary Authors*, New Revision Series, vol. 19, 369.

14. Peck, "The Genteel Unshelving of a Book," 37–38.

15. Henke, "The Death of the Mother," 34.

16. Peck, "People of the Word," 20.

17. Peck, "The Invention of Adolescence," 186.

18. Ibid.

19. Betty Cuniberti, "Author's Book Explores What Teen-age Boys Are Made Of," *Los Angeles Times*, 14 November 1982, 20.

20. *Bulletin of the Center for Children's Books*, November 1981, 53.

21. Norma Bagnall, *The ALAN Review*, Winter 1982, 21.

22. Kay Webb O'Connel, *School Library Journal*, September 1981, 140.

23. Best Sellers, January 1982, 403.

24. Ann A. Flowers, *Horn Book*, July–August 1985, 457.

25. Mary R. Oran, *Book Report*, September–October 1985.

26. Cynthia K. Leibold, *School Library Journal*, April 1985, 99.

27. Hazel Rochman, *Booklist*, 1 March 1985, 945.

28. *Publishers Weekly*, 17 May 1985, 118.

29. Oran, *Book Report*.

30. John W. Conner and Kathleen N. Tessmer, "1986 Books for Young Adults Poll," *English Journal*, December 1986, 60.

31. Richard Peck, "Suicide as a Solution?," Dell Publishing Company publicity brochure, n.d.

32. Lenore Skenazy, *Advertising Age*, 18 April 1985, 13.

33. Kristiana Gregory, *Los Angeles Times Book Review*, 10 August 1986.

Chapter 9

1. Patty Campbell, *Wilson Library Bulletin*, October 1979, 122.

2. Joan Foster, *Danbury News-Times*, 3 February 1980.

3. Marilyn Kay, *School Library Journal*, November 1979, 92.

4. *Kirkus Reviews*, 15 October 1979, 1213.

5. Dave Davidson et al., *English Journal*, May 1980, 95.

6. Peck, Speech at Children's Literature Festival, University of Southern Mississippi.

7. Peck, quoted by Jean W. Ross, *Contemporary Authors*, New Revision Series, vol. 19, 368.

8. J. D. Reed, "Packaging the facts of Life," *Time*, 23 August 1982, 6.

9. Peck, workshop at Montclair (New Jersey) Public Library.

10. Ibid.

11. Janice K. Tovey, "Writing for the Young Adult Reader: An Analysis of Audience in the Novels of Richard Peck, master's thesis, Illinois State University, 1988, 82.

12. Carolyn Meyer, *Los Angeles Times*, 11 June 1987.

13. *Kirkus Reviews*, 1 May 1987, 724.

14. Evie Wilson, *Voice of Youth Advocates*, June 1987, 82.

Chapter 10

1. Rise Bill, *Best Sellers*, May 1980, 50.

2. Peck, quoted by Jean W. Ross, *Contemporary Authors*, New Revision Series, vol. 19, 368.

3. *Kirkus Reviews*, 1 January 1980, 32.

4. *Publishers Weekly*, 18 January 1980, 130.

5. Richard Peck, interviewed by Jean F. Mercier, *Publishers Weekly*, 14 March 1980.

6. Jane Langton, *Washington Post*, 23 March 1980, 12.

7. Joni Bodart, "The Also-Rans; or 'What Happened to the Ones That Didn't Get Eight Votes?'" *Top of the News*, Fall 1981, 72.

8. Peck, quoted by Jean W. Ross, *Contemporary Authors*, New Revision Series, vol. 19, 368.

9. Kate Waters, *School Library Journal*, March 1981, 161–62.

10. *Publishers Weekly*, 23 January 1981, 120.

11. *Kirkus Reviews*, 1 January 1981, 35.

12. Susan Branch, *Library Journal*, 1 February 1981, 370.

13. Stoddard Martin, "Knights in Blue Denim," *Times Literary Supplement*, 21 August 1981, 966.

14. Stephanie Zvirin, *Booklist*, 1 July 1981, 1388.

15. Jane Howard, *Mademoiselle*, March 1981, 70.

16. Peck, quoted by Jean W. Ross, *Contemporary Authors*, New Revision Series, vol. 19, 368–69.

17. Peck, interview at Montclair (New Jersey) Public Library.

18. Cathie Lou Porrelli, "El Monte Pioneers' Tale Told in New Novel," *San Gabriel Valley Tribune*, 16 June 1983.

19. Diana Ketcham, "Rediscovering San Simeon's Architect," *New York Times*, 28 April 1988.

20. Mary Sucher, *The ALAN Review*, Spring 1984, 33.

21. Sarah McGowan, *Best Sellers*, May 1983, 44–45.

22. Stephanie Zvirin, *Booklist*, 1 February 1983, 698.

23. John W. Connor et al., "1984 Books for Young Adults Poll," *English Journal*, December 1984, 64.

Chapter 11

1. Lloyd Cooper, Maple Valley High School, Michigan, May 1987.

2. Patty Campbell, *Wilson Library Bulletin*, January 1985, 341.

3. Lola H. Teabert, *Voice of Youth Advocates*, February 1988, 284.

4. *Kirkus Reviews*, 1 May 1977, 485.

5. Janet French, *School Library Journal*, September 1977, 113.

6. Ruth M. Stein, *Language Arts*, January 1978, 46.

7. *Publishers Weekly*, 13 June 1977, 107.

Chapter 12

1. Tovey, *Writing for the Young Adult Reader*, 77.

2. Peck, interviewed by Paul Janeczko, *English Journal*, 97.

3. Peck, quoted by Jean W. Ross, *Contemporary Authors*, New Revision Series, vol. 19, 370.

4. Kenneth L. Donelson and Alleen Pace Nilsen, *Literature for Today's Young Adults* (Glenview, Ill.: Scott, Foresman Company, 1980), 19.

5. Tovey, *Writing for the Young Adult Reader*, 22.

6. Peck, interview at Montclair (New Jersey) Public Library.

Appendix B

1. Leonard Maltin, ed., *Leonard Maltin's TV Movies and Video Guide* (New York: New American Library, 1988), 40.

2. Steven H. Scheuer, *The Complete Guide to Videocassette Movies* (New York: Holt, Rinehart & Winston, 1987), 26.

3. Maltin, *Leonard Maltin's TV Movies and Video Guide*, 308.

4. Janet Seigel, "From Page to Screen: Where the Author Fits In," *Top of the News*, Spring 1984, 282.

5. Richard Peck, Speech at Central Connecticut State University, 9 April 1975.

6. Richard Peck, "People of the Word," 21.

7. M. D. Kramer, "A Bushel of Peck for Teens," *Boston Herald American*, 5 September 1982.

Selected Bibliography

Primary Works

Young Adult Novels

Are You in the House Alone? New York: Viking, 1976; Dell, 1977.
Blossom Culp and the Sleep of Death. New York: Delacorte, 1986; Dell, 1987.
Close Enough to Touch. New York: Delacorte, 1981; Dell, 1982, 1986.
Don't Look and It Won't Hurt. New York: Holt, Rinehart & Winston, 1972; Avon, 1973, 1979, 1983.
The Dreadful Future of Blossom Culp. New York: Delacorte, 1983; Dell, 1984, 1986, 1987.
Dreamland Lake. New York: Holt, Rinehart & Winston, 1973; Avon, 1974; Dell, 1982, 1986.
Father Figure. New York: Viking, 1978; New American Library, 1979; Dell, 1988.
The Ghost Belonged to Me. New York: Viking, 1975; Dell, 1976, 1986, 1987.
Ghosts I have Been. New York: Viking, 1977; Dell, 1979, 1986, 1987.
Princess Ashley. New York: Delacorte, 1987; Dell, 1988.
Remembering the Good Times. New York: Delacorte, 1985; Dell, 1986.
Representing Superdoll. New York: Viking, 1974; Avon, 1975, 1980; Dell, 1982, 1986.
Secrets of the Shopping Mall. New York: Delacorte, 1979; Dell, 1980, 1986.
Through a Brief Darkness. New York: Viking, 1973; Avon, 1974, 1981; Dell, 1982, 1986.
Those Summer Girls I Never Met. New York: Delacorte, 1988.

Adult Novels

Amanda/Miranda. New York: Viking, 1980; Avon, 1981.
This Family of Women. New York: Delacorte, 1983; Dell, 1984.
New York Time. New York: Delacorte, 1981; Dell, 1981.

Children's Picture Books

Monster Night at Grandma's House, illustrated by Don Freeman. New York: Viking, 1977.
What Ever Happened to Thanksgiving? Unpublished manuscript.

Edited Essay Collections

Edge of Awareness: Twenty-Five Contemporary Essays, with Ned E. Hoopes. New York: Dell, 1966.
Leap into Reality: Essays for Now. New York: Dell, 1973.

Edited Poetry Collections

Mindscapes: Poems for the Real World. New York: Delacorte, 1971; Dell, 1972.
Pictures That Storm Inside My Head: Poems for the Inner You. New York: Avon, 1976.
Sounds and Silences: Poetry for Now. New York: Delacorte, 1970; Dell, 1970; Avon, 1976.

Educational Books

A Consumer's Guide to Educational Innovations, with Mortimer Smith and George Weber. Washington, D.C.: Council for Basic Education, 1972.
The Creative Word vol. 2, with Stephen N. Judy. New York: Random House, 1973.
Open Court Correlated Language Arts Program. LaSalle, Ill.: Open Court Publishing Company, 1967.
Transitions: A Literary Paper Casebook (compiled). New York: Random House, 1974.
Urban Studies: A Research Paper Casebook (compiled). New York: Random House, 1973.

Self-published Book

Old Town: A Complete Guide: Strolling, Shopping, Supping, Sipping, 2nd ed., with Norman Strasma. Chicago, 1965.

Short Stories

"I Go Along." Unpublished manuscript.

"Priscilla and the Wimps." In *Sixteen: Short Stories by Outstanding Writers for Young Adults*, edited by Donald R. Gallo, 42–45. New York: Delacorte, 1984; Dell, 1985.

"Shadows." In *Visions: Nineteen Short Stories by Outstanding Writers for Young Adults*, edited by Donald R. Gallo, 2–9. New York: Delacorte, 1987; Dell, 1988.

"The Size of the Universe." *Southwest Review*, Autumn 1986, 493–509.

Poems

"Early Admission." Unprinted. Written 1971.

"The Geese." In *Sounds and Silences: Poetry for Now*, edited by Richard Peck, 9. New York: Delacorte, 1970.

"Irish Child." *Chicago Tribune Magazine*, 17 September 1972.

"Jump Shot." In *Mindscapes: Poems for the Real You*, edited by Richard Peck, 8. New York: Delacorte, 1971.

"Lesson in History." *Chicago Tribune Magazine*, 7 July 1974.

"Mission Uncontrolled." In *Mindscapes: Poems for the Real World*, edited by Richard Peck, 86–87. New York: Delacorte, 1971.

"Nancy." In "Phoenix Nest," edited by Martin Levin, *Saturday Review*, 21 June 1969, 6.

"Street Trio." In "Phoenix Nest," edited by Martin Levin, *Saturday Review*, 4 September 1971, 6.

"TKO." In *Sports Poems*, edited by R. R. Knudson and P. K. Ebert, 142. New York: Dell Publishing Company, 1971.

Essays

"Art Deco: The Newest 'Antique.'" *House Beautiful*, August 1973, 61–63.

"Can Students Evaluate Their Education?" *PTA Magazine*, February 1971, 4–7.

"Care and Feeding of the Visiting Author." *Top of the News*, Spring 1982, 251–55.

"Coming Full Circle: From Lesson Plans to Young Adult Novels." *Horn Book*, April 1985, 208–15.

"Consciousness-Raising." *American Libraries*, February 1974, 75–76.

"A Conversation with Richard Peck." Dell Publishing Company publicity brochure, n.d.

"Delivering the Goods." *American Libraries*, October 1974, 492–94.

Dell Publishing Company publicity brochure, November 1988, 6.

"An Exclusive Interview with Blossom Culp." Dell Publishing Company publicity brochure, 1987.

"From Realism to Melodrama." *American Libraries*, February 1975, 106–08.

"Future-Laugh." In "Phoenix Nest," edited by Martin Levin, *Saturday Review*, 26 August 1972, 69–70.

"The Genteel Unshelving of a Book." *School Library Journal*, May 1986, 37–39.

"Growing Up Suburban: 'We Don't Use Slang, We're Gifted.'" In "In the YA Corner," *School Library Journal*, October 1985, 118–19.

"In the Country of Teenage Fiction." *American Libraries*, April 1973, 204–07.

"The Invention of Adolescence and Other Thoughts on Youth." *Top of the News*, Winter 1983, 182–90.

"It's a World Away and Yet So Close." *New York Times*, 8 October 1972, 4, 12.

"Of Rabbits and Roadsters." *American Libraries*, July–August 1974, 360–61.

"People of the World: A Look at Today's Young Adults and Their Needs." *School Library Media Quarterly*, Fall 1981, 16–21.

"A Personal Letter from: Blossom Culp to: Whom It May Concern." Dell Publishing Company publicity brochure, n.d.

"Rape and the Teenage Victim." *Top of the News*, Winter 1978, 175–76.

"Richard Peck Discusses Adolescent Rape." Dell Publishing Company publicity release, n.d.

"Richard Peck Responds to National Book Week with 7 Do's and 7 Don'ts for Parents." Avon Books publicity release.

"Some Thoughts on Adolescent Lit." *News from ALAN*, September–October 1975, 4–7.

"St. Charles Is the Last Trolley Left." *New York Times*, 28 January 1973, 3, 17.

"Suicide as a Solution?" Dell Publishing Company publicity brochure, n.d.

"Teenagers' Tastes." *American Libraries*, May 1974, 235–36.

"Ten Questions to Ask about a Novel." *ALAN Newsletter*, Spring 1978, 1, 7. Viking Press publicity brochure, n.d.

"We Can Save Our Schools." *Parents' Magazine and Better Family Living*, September 1971, 51–52, 98–101.

"A Writer from Illinois." *Illinois Libraries*, June 1986, 392–94.

"YA Books in the Decade of the Vanishing Adult." *Dell Carousel*, Fall–Winter 1985–86, 1–2.

"Young Adult Books." *Horn Book*, September–October 1986, 619.

Prayers

"A Teenager's Prayer." in "Young Adult Books," *Horn Book*, September–October 1968, 621.

"The Fervent Prayer of a Teenager's Parent." *The ALAN Review*, Winter 1987, 51.

"A Teacher's Prayer," *News from Dell Books*, n.d.

Speeches

Speech at Central Connecticut State University, 9 April 1975.
Speech at the Children's Book Council / American Booksellers Association, New Orleans, 24 May 1986.
Speech at the Children's Literature Festival, University of Southern Mississippi, Hattiesburg, 19 March 1981.

Secondary Works

Books and Parts of Books

Commire, Anne, ed. *Something about the Author.* Vol. 18. Detroit: Gale Research Company, 1980, 242–44.
Donelson, Kenneth L., and Nilsen, Alleen Pace. *Literature for Today's Young Adults.* Glenview, Ill.: Scott, Foresman and Company, 1980.
Dust jacket for *Princess Ashley.* New York: Delacorte Press, 1987.
Gallo, Donald R., ed. *Speaking for Ourselves.* In preparation.
Gunton, Sharon R., ed. *Contemporary Literary Criticism,* vol. 21. Detroit: Gale Research Company, 1982, 295–301.
Locher, Frances Carol, ed. *Contemporary Authors,* 85–88. Detroit: Gale Research Company, 1980, 458–59.
Maltin, Leonard, editor. *Leonard Maltin's TV Movies and Video Guide,* 1988 edition. New York: New American Library, 1988.
Nilsen, Alleen Pace, and Donelson, Kenneth L. *Literature for Today's Young Adults.* 2nd ed. Glenview, Ill.: Scott, Foresman and Company, 1985.
Sarkissian, Adele, ed. *Something about the Author Autobiography Series.* Vol. 2. Detroit: Gale Research Company, 1985, 175–86.
Scheuer, Steven H. *The Complete Guide to Videocassette Movies.* New York: Holt, Rinehart & Winston, 1987.
Schwartz, Sheila. *Teaching Adolescent Literature: A Humanistic Approach.* Rochelle Park, N.J.: Hayden Book Company, 1979.
Tovey, Janice K. "Writing for the Young Adult Reader: An Analysis of Audience in the Novels of Richard Peck." Master's thesis, Illinois State University, 1988.

Articles

"Best of the Best Books 1970–82." *Booklist,* 15 October 1983, 351–54.
Bodart, Joni. "The Also-Rans; or 'What Happened to the Ones That Didn't Get Eight Votes?'" *Top of the News,* Fall 1981, 70–72.

Carlsen, G. Robert, Bennett, Connie, and Harker, Anne. "1977 Books for Young Adult Book Poll." *English Journal*, January 1978, 90–95.

Carlsen, G. Robert, Manna, Tony, and Yoder, Jan. "1975 BYA Book Poll." *English Journal*, January 1976, 95–99.

Connor, John W., et al. "1984 Books for Young Adults Poll." *English Journal*, December 1984, 64–68.

Connor, John W., and Tessmer, Kathleen. "1986 Books for Young Adults Poll." *English Journal*, December 1986, 58–61.

Crew, Hilary. "Blossom Culp and Her Ilk: The Independent Female in Richard Peck's YA Fiction." *Top of the News*, Spring 1987, 297–301.

Cuniberti, Betty. "Author's Book Explores What Teen-age Boys Are Made Of." *Los Angeles Times*, 14 November 1982, part 6.

Elleman, Barbara. "50 Books Too Good to Be Missed." *Learning*, April–May 1985, 24–28.

Gallo, Donald R. "Who Are the Most Important YA Authors?" *The ALAN Review*, Spring 1989, 18–20.

Henke, James T. "The Death of the Mother, the Rebirth of the Son: *Millie's Boy* and *Father Figure*," *Children's Literature in Education*, Spring 1983, 21–34.

Jankowski, Jane. "Books Spur Complaints." *Decatur Herald and Review*, 11 March 1986.

Ketcham, Diana. "Rediscovering San Simeon's Architect." *New York Times*, 28 April 1988.

Kramer, M. D. "A Bushel of Peck for Teens." *Boston Herald American*, 5 September 1982.

Porrelli, Cathie Lou. "El Monte Pioneers' Tale Told in New Novel." *San Gabriel Valley Tribune*, 16 June 1983.

Reed, J. D. "Packaging the Facts of Life." *Time*, 23 August 1982, 65–66.

"Richard Peck: Right for All Ages, Writing for All Ages." *Openers*, Summer 1982.

Schleler, Curt. "Peck Is Author Whose Dreams Came True." *Grand Rapids Press*, 25 July 1982.

Seigel, Janet. "From Page to Screen: Where the Author Fits In." *Top of the News*, Spring 1984, 282–83.

Smith, Patrice. "Author Aims at Teen-age Ideals." *Evansville Courier*, 1986.

Sulkin, Randi. "Richard Peck: Writing Is Communication." *Ketchikan Daily News*, 3–9 March 1984, 2.

"Tips That Get Kids Reading." *Ketchikan Daily News*, 3–9 March 1984, 3.

Interviews

"An Interview with Richard Peck." *Scholastic Voice*, 6 September 1985, 12–13.

Gallo, Donald R. Interview with Nancy Gallt (telephone), 22 July 1988.
————. Interview with Richard Peck (tape recording), Montclair (New Jersey) Public Library, 9 December 1987.
Janeczko, Paul. "An Interview with Richard Peck." *English Journal*, February 1976, 97–99.
————. Interview with Richard Peck. In *From Writers to Students: The Pleasures and Pains of Writing*, edited by M. Jerry Weiss, 79–83. Newark, Del.: International Reading Association, 1979.
Mercier, Jean F. "PW Interviews Richard Peck." *Publishers Weekly*, 14 March 1980, 6–7.
Ross, Jean W. "CA Interview." *Contemporary Authors*. New Revision Series, vol. 19, edited by Linda Metzger. Detroit: Gale Research Company, 1987, 367–70.
Stanek, Lou Willett. "Just Listening: Interviews with Six Adolescent Novelists: Patricia McKillip, Robert Cormier, Norma Klein, Richard Peck, S. E. Hinton, Judy Blume." *Arizona English Bulletin*, April 1976, 23–38.

Speeches

Workshop at Montclair (New Jersey) Public Library, 9 December 1987. Tape recording.

Letter

Cooper, Lloyd. Maple Valley High School, Michigan. Letter to Donald R. Gallo, May 1987.

Selected Book Reviews

Amanda/Miranda
Bill, Rise. *Best Sellers*, May 1980, 50.
Kirkus Reviews, 1 January 1980, 32.
Langten, Jane. *Washington Post*, 23 March 1980, 12.
Publishers Weekly, 18 January 1980, 130.

Are You in the House Alone?
Heins, Paul. *Horn Book*, February 1977, 60.
Kirkus Reviews, 1 September 1976, 982.
Leonberger, Janet. *Young Adult Cooperative Book Review Group of Massachusetts*, February 1977, 89–90.

Levy, J. W. *Journal of Reading,* April 1978, 655.
Nelson, Alix. *New York Times Book Review,* 14 November 1976, 29.
Sutherland, Zena. *Bulletin of the Center for Children's Books,* March 1977, 111-12.

Blossom Culp and the Sleep of Death
Campbell, Patty. *Wilson Library Bulletin,* March 1986, 51.
Cart, Michael. *School Library Journal,* May 1986, 108.
Levine, Susan. *Voice of Youth Advocates,* June 1986, 82.
Publishers Weekly, 21 March 1986.

Close Enough to Touch
Bagnall, Norma. *The ALAN Review,* Winter 1982, 21.
Best Sellers, January 1982, 403.
Bulletin of the Center for Children's Books, November 1981, 53.
Chelton, Mary K. *Voice of Youth Advocates,* October 1981, 36.
Davis, Paxton. *New York Times Book Review,* 15 November 1981, 56, 69.
O'Connell, Kay Webb. *School Library Journal,* September 1981, 140.
Publishers Weekly, 2 October 1981, 111.

Don't Look and It Won't Hurt
Booklist, 15 February 1973, 574.
Kirkus Reviews, 15 August 1972, 949.
Pogrebin, Letty Cottin. *New York Times Book Review,* 12 November 1972, 8, 10, 14.
Publishers Weekly, 25 September 1972, 60.
Sullivan Peggy. *Library Journal,* 15 December 1972, 4080.

The Dreadful Future of Blossom Culp
Crompton, Anne Eliot. *Parents' Choice,* Spring–Summer 1984, 5.
Gauch, Patricia Lee. *New York Times Book Review,* 18 December 1987, 21.
Heins, Ethel L. *Horn Book,* February 1984, 64.
Ocala Star Banner, 25 December 1984.
Sorenson, Marilou. *Deseret News,* 29 January 1984.
Williamson, Susan H. *Kliatt Young Adult Paperback Book Guide,* October 1984, 4.

Dreamland Lake
Booklist, 15 November 1973, 342.
Kirkus Reviews, 15 June 1973, 648.
New York Times Book Review, 13 January 1974, 10.
Publishers Weekly, 6 August 1973, 65.
School Library Journal, December 1976, 69.

Sutherland, Zena. *Bulletin of the Center for Children's Books*, January 1974, 83–84.
Yucht, Alice H. *School Library Journal*, 15 November 1973, 53.

Father Figure
Booklist, 15 July 1978, 1728.
Kirkus Reviews, 1 September 1978, 953.
Pollack, Pamela D. *School Library Journal*, October 1978, 158.
Publishers Weekly, 17 July 1978, 168.
Rosen, Winifred. *Washington Post Book World*, 12 November 1978, E4.
Top of the News, Fall 1980, 62.

The Ghost Belonged to Me
Atwater, Judith. *School Library Journal*. September 1975, 109.
Booklist, 1 July 1975, 1129.
Clements, Bruce. *Psychology Today*, September 1975, 11, 75.
Junior Bookshelf, June 1977, 182–83.
Kirkus Reviews, 15 April 1975, 456.
Levine, Joan Goldman. *New York Times Book Review*, 27 July 1975, 8.

Ghosts I Have Been
Heins, Ethel L. *Horn Book*, February 1978, 56.
Jackson, Jane B. *Kliatt Young Adult Paperback Book Guide*, Fall 1979, 10, 12.
Kirkus Reviews, 15 September 1977, 991.
Manna, Tony. *The ALAN Review*, Fall 1979.
Milton, Joyce. *New York Times Book Review*, 30 October 1977, 34.
Publishers Weekly, 11 July 1977, 81.
Silver, Linda. *School Library Journal*, November 1977, 61.

Mindscapes: Poems for the Real World
Booklist, 15 July 1971, 952.
Clemons, Walter. *New York Times Book Review*, 27 June 1971, 8.
Dorsey, Margaret A. *Library Journal*, 15 June 1971, 2140.
Kirkus Reviews, 1 March 1971, 244.

Monster Night at Grandma's House
French, Janet. *School Library Journal*, September 1977, 113.
Kirkus Reviews, 1 March 1977, 485.
Publishers Weekly, 13 June 1977, 107.
Stein, Ruth M. *Language Arts*, January 1978, 45–46.

New York Time
Branch, Susan. *Library Journal*, 1 February 1981, 370.

Howard, Jane. *Mademoiselle*, March 1981, 70.
Kirkus Reviews, 1 January 1981, 35.
Martin, Stoddard. "Knights in Blue Denim," *Times Literary Supplement*, 21 August 1981, 966.
Publishers Weekly, 23 January 1981, 120.
Waters, Kate. *School Library Journal*, March 1981, 161–62.
Zvirin, Stephanie. *Booklist*, 1 July 1981, 1388.

Pictures That Storm Inside My Head: Poems for the Inner You
Booklist, 1 December 1976, 532–33.
Marks, Sarajean. *School Library Journal*, May 1977, 71.
Sorensen, Marilou. *Deseret News*, Fall 1981.

Princess Ashley
Anton, Denise A. *School Library Journal*, August 1987, 97.
Kirkus Reviews, 1 May 1987, 723–24.
Meyer, Carolyn. *Los Angeles Times*, 11 July 1987.
Publishers Weekly, 29 May 1987, 79.
School Library Journal, December 1987, 38.
Wilson, Evie. *Voice of Youth Advocates*, June 1987, 82.

"Priscilla and the Wimps"
Campbell, Patty. *Wilson Library Bulletin*, January 1985, 341.

Remembering the Good Times
Bodart, Joni. *Voice of Youth Advocates*, 15 June 1985, 134.
Brewbaker, Jim. *The ALAN Review*, Winter 1987, 33.
Flowers, Ann A. *Horn Book*, July–August 1985, 457–58.
Gregory, Kristina. *Los Angeles Times Book Reviews*, 10 August 1986.
Leibold, Cynthia K. *School Library Journal*, April 1985, 99.
Oran, Mary R. *Book Report*, September–October 1985.
Publishers Weekly, 17 May 1985, 118.
Skenazy, Lenore. *Advertising Age*, 18 April 1985, 13.
Rochman, Hazel. *Booklist*, 1 March 1985, 945.

Representing Superdoll
Alexander, Jean. *Washington Post Book World*, 10 November 1974, 8.
Booklist, 1 October 1974, 158–59.
Publishers Weekly, 9 September 1974, 68.
Sutherland, Zena. *Bulletin of the Center for Children's Books*, November 1974, 51.
Wheatley, Bonnie R. *School Library Journal*, October 1974, 120.

Secrets of the Shopping Mall
Campbell, Patty. *Wilson Library Bulletin*, October 1979, 12–13.
Davidson, Dave, et al. *English Journal*, May 1980, 94–95.
Foster, Joan. *Danbury News-Times*, 3 February 1980.
Kay, Marilyn. *School Library Journal*, November 1979, 92.
Kirkus Reviews, 15 October 1979, 1213.
McBroom, Gerry. *The ALAN Review*, Spring 1980, 19.
Sutherland, Zena. *Bulletin of the Center for Children's Books*, February 1980, 115.

"Shadows"
Teabert, Lola H. *Voice of Youth Advocates*, February 1988, 284–85.

Sounds and Silences: Poetry for Now
Booklist, 1 November 1970, 224.
Christian Science Monitor, 27 January 1971.
Conner, John W. *English Journal*, September 1971, 829–30.
Saturday Review, 19 September 1970, 35.
Seacord, Laura F. *Library Journal*, 15 November 1970, 4058.

This Family of Women
Block, Marylaine. *Library Journal*, 15 February 1983, 413–14.
Clancy, Cathy. *School Library Journal*, May 1983, 97.
Kirkus Reviews, 1 February 1983, 142–43.
McGowan, Sarah. *Best Sellers*, May 1983, 44–45.
Sucher, Mary. *The ALAN Review*, Spring 1984, 33.
Zvirin, Stephanie. *Booklist*, 1 February 1983, 698.

Through a Brief Darkness
Fisher, Margery. *Growing Point*, April 1976, 2844–48, in *Contemporary Literary Criticism*, vol. 21, edited by Sharon R. Gunton (Detroit: Gale Research, 1982), 298.
Junior Bookshelf, October 1976, 183.
Kirkus Reviews, 1 December 1973, 1314.
Sullivan, Peggy. *School Library Journal*, 15 February 1974, 582.

Index

About the Author

Donald R. Gallo is professor of English at Central Connecticut State University where he supervises student teachers in English and teaches a course in literature for young adults and courses in writing, for teachers as well as for students. Gallo has been president of the Assembly on Literature for Adolescents of the National Council of Teachers of English, vice-chair of the Conference on English Education, a member of the NCTE Editorial Board, and editor of the *Connecticut English Journal*.

In addition to editing the 1985 edition of NCTE's *Books for You*, Gallo is editor of *Sixteen* and *Visions*, two collections of short stories written by well-known authors of young adult novels, and compiler of a forthcoming book of autobiographies of one hundred young adult authors. His articles have appeared in the *English Journal, Journal of Reading, School Library Journal, American Libraries, Research in the Teaching of English*, and other educational publications.